ACKNOWLEDGING THE PROPHETIC

A Personal Journey of Experiencing and Understanding the Prophetic Gift

BILL ARNOLD

ACKNOWLEDGING THE PROPHETIC
Copyright © 2023 by Bill Arnold
ISBN: 978-1-949297-68-3
LCCN: 2023923076

All rights reserved. No part of this book may be reproduced, stored in a retrieval system, or transmitted in any form or by any means—electronic, mechanical, digital, photocopy, or any other—without prior permission from the publisher and author, except as provided by the United States of America copyright law.

Unless otherwise noted, all scriptures are from THE HOLY BIBLE, ENGLISH STANDARD VERSION®, Copyright© 2001 by Crossway, a publishing ministry of Good News Publishers. Used by permission.

Scripture quotations marked (NASB) are taken from the NEW AMERICAN STANDARD BIBLE®, Copyright© 1960, 1962, 1963, 1968, 1971, 1972, 1973, 1975, 1977, 1995 by The Lockman Foundation. Used by permission.

Scripture quotations marked (NKJV) are taken from the NEW KING JAMES VERSION®. Copyright© 1982 by Thomas Nelson, Inc. Used by permission. All rights reserved.

Scripture quotations marked (KJV) are taken from the KING JAMES VERSION, public domain.

Address all personal correspondence to:
Bill Arnold
billarnoldhome@gmail.com

Individuals and church groups may order books from Bill Arnold directly, or from the publisher. Retailers and wholesalers should order from our distributors. Refer to the Deeper Revelation Books website for distribution information, as well as an online catalog of all our books.

Editorial Consultant: Jonathan Beard

Published by:
Deeper Revelation Books
Revealing "the deep things of God" (1 Cor. 2:10)
P.O. Box 4260
Cleveland, TN 37320 423-478-2843
Website: www.deeperrevelationbooks.org
Email: info@deeperrevelationbooks.org

Deeper Revelation Books assist Christian authors in publishing and distributing their books. Final responsibility for design, content, permissions, editorial accuracy, and doctrinal views, either expressed or implied, belongs to the author. What you hold in your hands (or what you are viewing in an e-book format) is an expression of this author's passion to publish the truth with a spirit of excellence. It was a blessing and an honor to help in the process.

Acknowledgements

I absolutely must give my appreciation and thanks to the following people who have influenced and touched my life with wisdom, counsel, and direction.

To Albie Pearson (Sept. 12, 1934–Feb. 20, 2023), a true-to-life apostle.

Albie and his wife Helen were biblical pastors, teachers, and founders of countless ministries, churches, and missions dedicated to the education and training of the five-fold ministry gifts. Albie was the founding pastor who set me on the road into the kingdom of God.

To Eric Stovesand (Sept. 20, 1950–Aug. 25, 2018), a man of incredible love, grace, wisdom, and balance.

Eric was my pastor and guide through my early years of understanding Jesus and God the Father. He taught me principles for how to study the Bible.

To Paul Morgan and Bruce Stefanik, two pastors who taught me, believed in me, and gave me opportunity in ministry.

They guided me through some very difficult life challenges and stood by my side with love, wisdom, and a firm hand to keep me aligned with God's Word and call on my life.

To Loren Cunningham and Youth With A Mission, University of the Nations, Hawaii.

Through YWAM, I experienced international missions and cultures, and through U of N and its incredible classes,

I gained an education of the Bible. "Know God and Make Him Known."

To the countless people who gave their time, energy, and love to walk with me, encourage me, and stand by my side.

To my five accountability partners: You know who you are.

You hold my feet to the fire. You ask me the tough questions. You teach me, you care about me, and you look out for me. And you listen to my wild and crazy adventures.

I also thank my wife and family as well as the people involved in helping me put this little book together. I pray to the Lord that He finds a good use for it and that it is helpful to anyone who is struggling to understand more about the gifts of the prophetic.

Now concerning spiritual gifts, brethren, I do not want you to be ignorant: You know that you were Gentiles, carried away to these dumb idols, however you were led. Therefore I make known to you that no one speaking by the Spirit of God calls Jesus accursed, and no one can say that Jesus is Lord except by the Holy Spirit.

There are diversities of gifts, but the same Spirit. There are differences of ministries, but the same Lord. And there are diversities of activities, but it is the same God who works all in all. But the manifestation of the Spirit is given to each one for the profit of all: for to one is given the word of wisdom through the Spirit, to another the word of knowledge through the same Spirit, to another faith by the same Spirit, to another gifts of healings by the same Spirit, to another the working of miracles, to another prophecy, to another discerning of spirits, to another different kinds of tongues, to another the interpretation of tongues. But one and the same Spirit works all these things, distributing to each one individually as He wills.

1 Corinthians 12:1–11 (NKJV)

Table of Contents

Introduction 11

CHAPTER 1
My Journey Begins 15

CHAPTER 2
My Early Christian Experience 21

CHAPTER 3
God Is a Communicator 29

CHAPTER 4
Qualifications of a Biblical Prophet 45

CHAPTER 5
Maturing Prophetically 57

CHAPTER 6
Experiences and Foundations 67

CHAPTER 7
Public Prophecies in the Church 73

CHAPTER 8
Experiencing Prophecy 83

CHAPTER 9
Hearing and Speaking 91

CHAPTER 10
Prayer and the Prophet 95

CHAPTER 11
The New Testament Prophet 103

CHAPTER 12
Non-Prophet Prophecies 113

CHAPTER 13
Continuing with My Prophetic Gift 121

FINAL THOUGHTS
Where Do We Go from Here? 127

Endnotes 129

Additional Resosurces for Further Study 131

About the Author 133

Introduction

Picture yourself walking through the desert with a dry tongue and a thirst to quench. You spot a small pool of clear, clean water. "Aah," you think, "something to quench my thirst!" You start to realize it won't sustain you for the long term, so you grab your tools and decide to dig down until you discover the wellspring. Then, it gushes forth.

I wrote this book to inspire you. If you don't find what you're looking for, grab your tools and dig a little deeper on the points that interest you. The spring of life is eternal and infinite, and, as believers, we have access to God for knowledge, wisdom, and revelation.

As I look at the current events in our world and continue to learn God's perspective, I often wonder if we are ready for what He has in store. Within America, we are a land full of controversy, division, lawlessness, and irrational ideologies that are becoming violent. Although not new to our world, these things are becoming more intense, exponentially accelerating at an alarming rate.

The intolerance for righteousness in our society has reached new heights.

In these last days before Christ's return, an interesting phenomenon is happening. As society is crumbling, it is also making new biblical discoveries, hidden since ancient times.

God is opening people's eyes and spiritual understanding to greater depths. For so many years, the church has been through social upheavals, language changes, cultural pressures, and divisions over doctrines. In its current state, the church is poorly educated in a biblical sense and easily moving forward in what the world often refers to as being "progressive." I fear the truth of God's Word has been so watered down and reinterpreted with the modern Western worldview that many no longer have a clue of the writer's view and intent.

From the beginning of my life when I accepted Christ as my Savior, I've sought after God and searched the Bible with questions. I have found many answers by dedicating myself to understanding the author's original context and culture.

To aid in my journey and feed my desperation to learn and experience more, I chose to enroll at University of the Nations (a Christian university developed from Youth With A Mission) in Biblical Studies, an intense inductive study of the Bible. Briefly stated, an inductive study is done without outside commentary sources. Only historical and cultural writings of the days the text was written are allowed. Essentially, inductive study uses the historical context to interpret and fill in what the author was experiencing at the time. Thus, the Bible would have to prove itself to be true to its own writings and doctrines.

That course changed my life and gave me the tools to discover biblical truth from the Word. Even though that course only scratched the surface, it was a gateway for me to study, learn, and experience God's truth. My approach to understanding Scripture and prophecy, the theme of this book, takes into account this inductive study of God's Word as well as some perspectives given by others with the same manner of study.

The following chapters are a personal account and journey of discovering, learning, and maturing in a gift God chose to share with me called the prophetic.

CHAPTER 1

My Journey Begins

The Formative Years

"You can refer to a person's experience of changing or developing from one state of mind to another as a journey."[1]

My journey began as a child raised in a non-Christian home living with an alcoholic father who was verbally abusive. The day came when the abuse became physical toward my mother, and she immediately took my older brother and me out of that situation. She divorced my father when I was five.

It's no secret divorce affects everyone differently. For me, it left a void in my life. The absence of my father created difficulties for me. As I emotionally processed the changes, I began to search for ways to be accepted, feel safety, and avoid rejection. For my personality, it meant looking for ways to escape the reality of my feelings—feelings like rejection.

When I was in the first and second grades, my mother was often called in for teacher's conferences to discuss why Billy was not doing well in school. The comment she most often heard was, "He's a daydreamer, always looking out the window and not paying attention in class." Of course, it was true! It was my only means of escape. It was me looking for something outside the normal, everyday life my young mind was trying to process. I realize now I never felt understood.

Even though my thoughts were always roaming, my belief in God was always present. I don't know why or where it came from. Perhaps it was from my praying grandmother. She would dress up every Sunday and take her baked goods to church, believing God would bless her for serving. Her belief must have made a mark on my mind.

I would talk to God like I was talking to an imaginary friend. I had absolutely no knowledge, information, teaching, or influence from others as it related to God, at least that I can remember. My family never outwardly expressed belief in anything spiritual.

By the time I was in middle school, I had been encouraged by an art teacher, who could see I was quite melancholy, to try expressing my thoughts and desires through drawing and other forms of fine arts. With that encouragement, I developed a natural gift, and my artistic talent gave me the escape I needed. I could just create my own world on paper or canvas.

My artistic accomplishments opened a way for me to be accepted and recognized, but the truth is, I still did not feel I was understood by others, and I was never satisfied with my life. I still gave into times of depression, melancholy, and a doubtful outlook for my future. I simply had an emptiness that wasn't being filled.

My mind began to think spiritually about things, and I wondered what might be on the other side of this earthly realm. I never looked at it as suicidal thoughts. I always looked at it like wanting to find a way out of my depressing circumstances by exploring a new world. And perhaps I'm stretching the idea a bit, but I can say I have always been drawn to explore.

Developing My Intrinsic Nature

I managed to maneuver my way through high school with a 1.5 GPA. I think it was the mercy of the school that advanced me through, or perhaps they didn't want to deal with me for another year. Nevertheless, I was out of high school and had to decide what to do next. I did the only thing logical to me: I managed to convince my mom and new stepdad to help with funds to enter college for none other than an art degree.

For financial reasons I had to stay within our state, so I chose the school furthest from home. Who at that age wants to be near their parents? If you're curious, I attended the University of Wisconsin—Superior. For me, it was all about getting away from home and finding ways to escape from reality.

I can look back and understand how God was developing my intrinsic nature as my life progressed over the years by using my innate desire to seek a world outside what I could see and understand. God arranged things to guide me toward Him and the unique spiritual gift He would use some day. I had challenges emotionally, educationally, and even physically that were part of shaping me to become the person He desired to be in relationship with.

God Caught My Attention

Attending classes at UWS was not my triumphant shift to greatness. I followed the traditional path of the typical college student. The only thing I wanted to do was go to art class and party. As a result, I walked the edge of suspension and expulsion due to failing grades. And my failure eventually ensued.

Before I left college, a shift to greatness did begin in my life aside from my failing grades. Not my greatness, but the greatness of God.

On one particularly cold winter day, I took a brisk, two-mile walk to the city post office to collect my mail. While on this walk, in my typical daydream state of mind, someone approached me from behind and tapped me on the shoulder. When I turned, I was only met by a cold breeze.

Considering my state of mind, I brushed it off and continued on. Yet again, the tap came. I continued ignoring it. Yet a third time, the tap came, and I blurted out loud, "What, God? What do You want?"

I surprised myself at my own response. I didn't even know what I was really asking. But there it was. Those words had just come out of my mouth.

> *With my response came the spark of a new journey. Who is God?*

With my response came the spark of a new journey. Who is God? That weekend, my college roommate left town. I was alone in the dorm room, so I watched TV, staying up as late as I wanted. In doing so, I encountered the TV movie-of-the-night called *The Exorcist*. Quite frankly, parts of it made me laugh, parts made me question, and parts made me angry.

The anger came when the movie showed the devil with so much power and control that he could take over the young girl. Why was I angry? I would suggest it was in part due to the intrinsic nature God had been developing in me.

I noticed my roommate had a Good News Bible on his shelf, and without realizing what I was doing, I decided to read what it had to say about all this. From Friday evening to Monday morning, I spent reading from the first page of Matthew to the end of Revelation. That was my first encounter with the Bible.

Looking back, I can confidently say I have both learned and experienced Isaiah 55:11, which says God's Word never comes back void: "So shall my word be that goes out from my mouth; it shall not return to me empty, but it shall accomplish that which I purpose, and shall succeed in the thing for which I sent it." Reading that Bible stirred my mind and heart, and God would not let me rest without discovering more.

Jumping ahead with a very short version of the next year, I left school without a degree and traveled across the country to Tahoe, CA. I was in search of God and Jesus, wanting to know who they really were. As far as family was concerned, I told them I went for a job at a ski resort. My salvation testimony is another story. For me to stay on task with the subject of this book, I need to jump ahead. About two months later, I walked into a nondenominational church, where I officially, publicly, gave my life to Jesus.

CHAPTER 2

My Early Christian Experience

About two months after my conversion, I began attending a small, nondenominational church with about 200 believers that today would be called a charismatic church. At the time, I knew very little about denominations. I had heard of the well-established, mainstream ones like Methodist, Baptist, Presbyterian, Catholic, etc. At that time in my walk, I could not reconcile the differences or why there would be any denominations. It simply seemed to me that if someone loved Jesus and believed the Bible, then why are denominations all so different? I rationalized that a nondenominational church made the most sense.

The church I attended in the beginning of my new walk with Jesus had a pastor named Eric. He took me under his arm to help me learn, grow, and understand Christianity by teaching me how to study the Bible and the character of God, as well as the gifts the Lord gives, both natural and spiritual ones.

Regarding the gifts, Pastor Eric explained 1 Corinthians 12:7–11 to me:

> *But to each one is given the manifestation of the Spirit for the common good. For to one is given the word of wisdom through the Spirit, and to another the word of knowledge according to the same Spirit; to another faith by the same Spirit, and to another gifts of healing by the one Spirit, and to another the effecting of miracles, and*

to another prophecy, and to another the distinguishing of spirits, to another various kinds of tongues, and to another the interpretation of tongues. But one and the same Spirit works all these things, distributing to each one individually just as He wills. (NASB)

As a new Christian, I was eager to understand what these gifts meant, how they are used, and if I was a candidate for any of them. But first things first—I needed someone's guidance. I decided to attend a small group from the church; we called them life groups.

In my life group, Eric was the leader. A typical meeting would include a couple people that would always begin with praying in a different language called tongues. Later, I learned more about this and how it might make a difference in how a person prays. However, at the time I didn't really comprehend how someone might receive that gift or what its function was.

Interestingly enough, God had His own plan on how to help me with that. I had attended the church for a few months when Pastor Eric realized I had not been water baptized. He immediately arranged to have me dunked like I had seen them do to others.

Yet, my baptism was unique as it was winter, and the baptism would be outdoors. It took place at a beautiful, two-story log home built near the base of Mount Houghton, overlooking the tall pines and Lake Tahoe. On the deck, the outdoor hot tub was giving off steam while the snow was falling. I looked forward to the event because it meant so much to be able to declare to the five Christian friends with me that I was truly committed to following Jesus. Little did I know that my commitment, which started in a hot tub, represented a depth of faith that would keep me moving forward and never turning back.

My First Supernatural Experience

There I was, with water up to my waist, thinking about how Jesus went into the grave and how I would be symbolizing the same action. Eric, holding my hand over my nose, spoke words over me about the Father, Son, and Holy Spirit. As my hearing went deaf, I fell backward into the pool of warm water rushing over me. The moments felt like slow motion, and in my mind, I declared to Jesus right there, "I'm all Yours forever!"

Then, just as Eric lifted me back up from the water, someone shined a bright, blinding light in my face. But no one there had a light! I began to verbally pray and praise, but something was different. I was speaking, but I did not recognize the words. It was my voice, but nothing I understood. I could hear my friends laughing a bit, and I could see their smiles. I looked at Eric for approval, and he simply said, "Let it flow, Bill, just let it flow." And so, I did.

Upon experiencing this new phenomenon, which was my first gift from the Holy Spirit, I pressed into gaining a thorough biblical understanding of the different manifestations and uses of tongues. I learned speaking in tongues is a gift that engages my spirit with His. In my experience, the gift of my prayer language greatly enhances the other gift that would follow.

What Is This Second Gift?

I continued to grow as a Christian, receiving more biblical teaching and more conviction to spread the Gospel. I had a hunger to know God that would not cease but continued to increase over the years. I wrote my own tracts and stood on the corner of town handing them out and engaging others in conversation. This went on for a few months. During that time, I never led anyone to Jesus personally, but something else did start to happen.

> I started to get visual pictures of things that seemed related to the conversations I was having with people on the street.

I started to get visual pictures of things that seemed related to the conversations I was having with people on the street. The visualizations were in the form of what I would call "insights." I asked myself if these experiences were just my imagination, or if something else is going on that the Holy Spirit was revealing to me.

As time went on, my street evangelism dwindled, and my involvement with our church became greater. I decided to serve in the lowest positions: I cleaned bathrooms, set up chairs, and did as much of the behind-the-scenes serving as I could. I truly did not want to be seen because I did not have the confidence to feel as though I had anything to offer other than my physical service. I continued to envision things quite vividly when I would pray with people, and then I began to have other seemingly spiritual experiences, such as dreams and visitations, that I will write about later.

Experimenting

As time went on and I was a few years older in my relationship with Jesus, my new gift of visual insight began to increase, however I seldom allowed it to be noticed by others.

In my small group setting, I spoke to Eric about it, and he looked at me very seriously with some hesitation. I did my best to explain, and fortunately, he was a very loving, wise, and open person to witness just what it was I was trying to explain. As I think back on that experience, I realize it was difficult to communicate what God was doing with me, and so I hoped to have some understanding and support to help me figure it out.

Eric was just that kind of guy. I can still remember him telling the life group of twelve people what I tried to explain to him. He said, "This is a safe place where we can discover things God wants us to learn and grow in and can even experiment or practice with one another. It's a place where we can assess each other's words and ideas by holding each other accountable to the Word of God, making sure we aren't going astray, whether it be in pride, arrogance, or simply a lack of understanding and knowledge."

Hearing his words, I felt an incredible amount of pressure and almost shut down because of my fear of being rejected. But he was right. I certainly didn't want to be doing something out of line with Scripture or God's will. And I didn't want to cause friction or harm. So I submitted to the group and Eric's leadership for instruction and accountability.

During that evening group time, someone finished praying, and then I stepped out and said what I was envisioning.

Then I prayed into that vision, meaning I used that vision to guide my prayer. Everyone had smiles that evening, and I felt good. I felt used by the Holy Spirit.

One week later, we met again, and I was excited to use this new gift that seemed to come so clearly to me. As the evening progressed, someone had a prayer request, and I spoke a word (as if from the Holy Spirit) that just seemed right. There was complete silence and maybe a cough.

I looked at Eric, and he looked a bit perplexed. "Uh oh," I thought to myself, "something is wrong." Then in his gentle and kind voice, Eric stepped up and asked the group, "What do we think of the word Bill just spoke?"

I gulped. And the responses stunned me a bit. "Well, can't really say that lines up biblically," one said. Another then said, "Not really sure where that came from." Still another said, "The manner with which that word was spoken just didn't resonate well." Finally, the death blow came: "Dude, that was way off!" Aaah! Ugh!

Needless to say, I was devastated, humiliated, and crushed. All those old feelings of rejection hit me hard, and I wanted to crawl under a rock. I debated if I should leave the group permanently or maybe even the church. All just from that one night. But Eric, being the sensitive man of God he was, saw immediately the effect it had on me and jumped in. He asked everyone to pray for me and not be critical of something like this new gift. He said that God was still teaching me and helping me to understand and grow in it.

And so, as a group, they asked me to stay committed to learning this gift. Eric used the example of learning an instrument. You don't always get it right from the beginning, but you also need accountability and instruction to grow with it until you have a good grasp and understanding of how it works.

I was very fortunate to have these kinds of foundational experiences with people that were mature in their faith, well versed in the Bible, and practicing the love of Christ.

All of these scenarios make up a brief history and bio of my early journey into discovering the realm of the prophetic. More of my experience will surface as we continue, but in the next chapter, I'm going to start introducing some biblical perspectives about and around the gift of prophecy.

CHAPTER 3

God Is a Communicator

To try to define prophecy, the prophetic nature, or prophetic giftings, I will first quote an often used phrase: "To begin, we need to start at the beginning." The obvious beginning is Genesis, chapter one.

Genesis 1:1 begins by saying, "In the beginning, God ..." The term here for "God" is the Hebrew *Elohim*. And the intention of the writer (Moses) is that this Elohim is the Most High God. Therefore, the capital "G" in God is noted, as opposed to a lower case "g" in reference to any god or gods. In verse three we read, "And God said ..." The lexicon in my Logos Bible Study Platform shows the word "said" in this verse is the Hebrew word *mĕrsay*, meaning "to mention, think, or command."[1]

Why is this discussion important to the gift of the prophetic? Because it shows that from the very beginning God speaks. He communicates. He is not silent; He has a voice. Whether you want to think His voice is audible or not is beside the point. We can take the simplest view of understanding that God speaks!

The next scriptural reference we'll look at is John 1:1–2: "In the beginning was the Word, and the Word was with God, and the Word was God. He was in the beginning with God."

In order to understand what this verse has to do with the prophetic, we must examine the phrase "the Word."

Let's dig in just a little bit. "Word" is the Greek word *logos*. In this verse's context, logos is a concept word used symbolically for the nature and function of Jesus Christ. "Word," or logos, also carries a concept and reference to the revelation of God to the world. Jesus was the incarnation or embodiment and revelation of God to our world.

When we talk about the prophetic, we have to consider an attribute connected to the very nature of God. He communicates to us through relationship, through which He reveals something about Himself. He didn't create us and remain silent! We need that communication from God for salvation, love, relating to others, and even our very life-or-death existence. God is a family person in every sense of the word. He created all of us to be family, along with all His heavenly hosts. In the beginning, we were all one big family together in Eden, where our Father, our Creator, walked among us.

> God is a family person in every sense of the word.

Because God is all about relationships, He chose to increase our ability to communicate with Him and for Him by extending extraordinary gifts and making them available to us as tools. Moses is a perfect example. He and God met together in the tabernacle (in the presence of God), and then Moses communicated to the people what God wanted to say. Over time, He orchestrated His people to keep written historical records such as the Dead Sea Scrolls, the Torah or Pentateuch (the first five books of the Bible), the Tanakh (a collection of ancient religious Hebrew writings by the Israelites), and the Septuagint, writings from the Second

Temple Judaism era. He inspired the biblical canon, and He chose to teach us through history about His spiritual gifts given by the Holy Spirit.

Prophecy Between the Testaments

God uses the gifts of all these written records, along with spiritual prophetic gifts and more, for our relationship with Him and His communication to all of us. Some people have been taught God was silent between the Old and New Testaments, from 450 BC to approximately 27 AD. These centuries mark the period between the time of the prophet Malachi and the time Jesus started His ministry in the book of Matthew.

Since God's entire involvement in our relationship depends on communication, do you think He decided to be mute for over 400 years? Did He only talk with His heavenly council and angels, thus cutting off all communication from mankind?

I suggest to you, God has never been silent, especially for 400 years! I wish people would stop teaching that. God spoke all throughout those 400 years, and plenty of His communication was through prophets and the prophetic presence of the Holy Spirit.

So, why don't we know about it then? For one, we discovered quite a bit when the Dead Sea Scrolls were found in 1947. The scrolls brought some minor corrections and confirmation to what we had through traditional historical means.

Do we have any proof of the prophetic words from God during those centuries? We do in the writings of Rabbi Akiba ben Joseph; John Hyrcanus I; Jesus, son of Ananias; Simon, a prophet leader; and Menahem. Also, from Scripture we see God speaking to Simeon in Luke 2:25–26, Anna in Luke 2:36, and, of course, John the Baptist, just to name a few. They were all prophets during this time of supposed silence.

We can understand more about this period relating to prophets. According to Jewish historical writings, prophecy was not suppressed; however, the Torah was heavily emphasized and prophecy de-emphasized. Harmony with the Torah was the focus. Eventually, the Jewish leaders, like the Pharisees, decided interpretation of the law should supersede both the prophetic office and the prophets' role. At that time, they considered the law to be far more superior to prophetic teaching. The recording of prophecy took a back seat to everything else.

I can imagine our adversary took great advantage of this focus on the law to try to stop people from hearing God speak through prophetic voices. Eventually, religious leaders became more and more divided into different groups, such as Essenes, Pharisees, Sadducees, and the Therapeutae.

The Essenes were quite apolitical and separated themselves from the other groups. They held onto the significance and importance of the prophetic and operated a school of prophecy.

Approximately 800–900 Dead Sea Scrolls and over 25,000 fragments are still being deciphered today. We don't yet know how much the Essenes or other groups knew about Jesus's arrival through foretelling or the prophetic because the Dead Sea Scrolls date the Essene sect to before the actual appearance of Christ, even though it had a few years of overlap. What we do know is the Essenes continued in the laws of Moses, not the law of grace or the new covenant of Christ.

It's important to have a well-rounded, biblical understanding of the prophetic. Therefore, we must examine the variations of the gift and service, both historically and in the present day. After all, our greatest focus and commitment is to be biblically sound and accurate in relating the truth of what the Most High is communicating.

What Are Biblical Prophets?

To be clear from the start, this is not meant to be, nor is it going to be, an exhaustive exposition of all the prophets of the Old and New Testament. Remember, drilling down is something I would encourage you to do.

When we look at a few points with biblical prophets, it is always good to ask a few questions. The first question should be this: What was the purpose or job of the biblical prophets?

The Old Testament records many prophetic people, male and female, named and unnamed, highly visible ones such as Moses, David, Solomon, Isaiah, Ezekiel, and Jeremiah, as well as less visible ones such as Hannah with her prophetic prayer. Frankly, the list of Old Testament prophets is very long. I'm sure you can find book volumes to study through them and extract all the qualities and nuances of each prophet. But if we take a high-altitude look, we can observe and make some general statements of what these prophets are doing and presenting.

Overall, we understand the prophets' writings were less focused on predictions or foretelling future events and much more focused on the sins of God's people: rebellion, worshiping false gods, and breaking promises made concerning their covenant with God. God spoke through the prophets to explain to the people what they must do to reestablish their position with God, which required them to repent of their rebellion. According to professor Dr. Michael S. Heiser, most biblical scholars generally refer to Old Testament prophets as "covenant enforcers."[2]

God wanted people to follow Him so He could eventually restore them to His original plan. However, widespread apostasy was a major reason why God often raised up prophets. They called attention to the people's failures and pronounced a judgment or an alternative. They also gave details of how those events would unfold. These were not human predictions but God's revelation. God, in His mercy, offered opportunities for the people to correct their ways.

> God wanted people to follow Him so He could eventually restore them to His original plan.

The early Hebrews, and later the Israelites, had serious problems following other gods. Books like Ezekiel describe the Israelites grossly perverting the altar in the temple with idols, horrifying objects, and disgusting rituals of worship and human sacrifice. God chose to divorce the Israelites. He evacuated the temple and then destroyed them, leaving only a small remnant of followers. (The books of Ezekiel and Jeremiah give pretty strong details of these events.)

The other message we can read very clearly in these same books is the revelation of the coming Messiah. Over and over, the details of Jesus Christ's arrival are outlined, described, and predicted.

When we read different prophetic books of the Bible and the events involving prophetic people, we can understand how the prophets preached the covenant to the people. Sometimes they preached for extended periods of time. Noah, who may have preached for 100 years before the flood actually came, was inspired by the revealed words or actions of the Holy Spirit in a predictive or prophetic message. That makes Noah a preacher and a prophet.

Noah is an example for us to recognize that even today preachers move in an authentic gift of prophecy at times. The very nature of preaching the Gospel is revealing the Word of God and can be described as prophetic in that sense. The Bible is inspired. Therefore, when preached and taught with the power of the Holy Spirit, direction, correction, encouragement, and understanding happen. This is prophetic in the sense that it restores people to a relationship with Jesus and brings a greater fulfillment of His new covenant with us.

Sometimes God communicated by the Spirit and at other times by an angelic presence or by writing on a wall or on tablets. Sometimes He spoke through men or women appointed by God as prophets. The purpose has always been to get us back into the family, to restore us back to the original relationship, which is also our final destiny, the New Eden, also called the New Earth. This refers to the final state of the kingdom of God when Christ returns and we are in our final, glorified state with our Creator. Isaiah 65:17 says:

> "For behold, I create new heavens and a new earth;
> And the former shall not be remembered or come to mind." (NKJV)

We should realize not all the prophets of the Bible only predicted the future. This is not to minimize the foretelling of events but to give us a fuller understanding of biblical prophecy. Foretelling is not what makes them or defines them as a prophet.

As an example, the psalms are filled with all kinds of prophetic revelation. David gets encouragement, direction, insight, enlightened understanding, and overwhelming waves of emotional conviction from God. His worship is so intense at times that language cannot even describe it. He himself finds that his words fail him to describe his experience in the presence of the Most High.

The Job of an Old Testament Prophet

I think we can safely say that a prophet spoke for God—he was God's mouthpiece. Living in a time of chaos or seeing chaos approach, the prophet was loyal to the true God, strongly convicted by the Abrahamic covenant (Genesis 12:1–3), and called to hold Israel accountable to it. They were expressing the voice and actions of God divinely revealed to them.

The words and actions of the prophet, male or female, moved people because they were inspired by the Spirit of God. It reunited people to their loyalty with God. Unfortunately, not all would believe or listen, and many would perish from God's judgment as a result. Essentially, the message to the people was to do and be what God wanted them to do and be.

Real Prophets and False Prophets

In the Old Testament culture, prophets would rise and fall, come and go, be true or false. God continually addressed these human inconsistencies that can cause confusion and incomplete messages. God gives His messages in a way that human nature won't interfere with what God is desiring to say to His people. And sometimes He repeats His messages through different prophets. This is definitely an eye-opener and should be taken seriously even to this day.

Consider that God had Jeremiah prophesy to Nebuchadnezzar in 605 BC, and two years after his prophecy, God appointed Daniel to release his prophetic word to Nebuchadnezzar. Then for several more years, Jeremiah continued his prophecies until suddenly, God also appointed Ezekiel to prophesy to Babylon, whose king was Nebuchadnezzar. God used this trio of prophets, who overlapped each other all the way to 536 BC. That was nearly seventy years of God using three different prophets in the same places at alternating times, addressing many of the same issues. Then, add to that mix false prophets such as Hananiah.

God laid down some ground rules for knowing which prophets are real and which are not. However, let's also consider the prophetic situation we are facing in our day since these rules still apply. It is not difficult to see in these last days the hundreds, perhaps thousands, of self-proclaimed prophets, seers, and those making predictions. I turn on YouTube and see at least twenty-five to fifty YouTube prophetic channels, all claiming to be from born-again, strong theological Christians who are proclaiming judgments, predicting politics, assessing the world, and more. The number of views for these channels are in the hundreds of thousands, with a few in the millions. People seem to clamor for their attention and will give their life savings to hear a word for their life that will give them hope for their future circumstances and direction for their jobs, love life, and happiness. I'm not saying they are all bad or wrong or crazy, but common sense says to pause and question who is real and who isn't.

Discerning all the prophetic voices out there can be head spinning. Who is actually speaking that word that is supposedly coming from God? Whom can you trust? We can still use two Old Testament biblical ways of discerning who is true and who is false today.

First, listen carefully, weighing out what is being said and holding it up to the Bible to make sure nothing is contrary to the true intent of the context. That means we need to actually read the Bible and have at least a basic understanding of its contextual intent. And yes, that means both the New and Old Testaments. Gaining this knowledge requires effort, time, and study. It is true you may be able to glean a great deal from some trustworthy teachers and preachers, but how will you know who they are? You have to apply yourself to the Word, and you must have the loyal commitment to Yahweh and understand His covenant with you through Jesus Christ.

For the following paragraph, I am paraphrasing the teaching found in chapters nine and ten of *How to Read the Bible for All Its Worth* by Gordon D. Fee and Douglas Stuart. In the Old Testament, a prophet would first present what appears as a lawsuit, containing a summons, charge, evidence, and verdict, though these elements may sometimes be implied rather than stated explicitly. Next would come an announcement of distress, the reason for distress, and a prediction of doom. Finally, the prophet would give a promise referring to the future and a mention of radical change or of a blessing. The prophets were not inspired to make any points or announce any doctrines not already contained in the Pentateuchal covenant.[3]

Another way to discern the true from the false is to see if the words spoken do or do not bear fruit. Do they come true? Do they bring enlightenment and greater understanding to the relationship with Christ? This method is a little more challenging in the case of a foretelling because the word could be for a later time, in which case you have to set it aside until the event reveals it. But understand the purpose of the delayed fulfillment of the prophecy may be for several reasons, one of which may be simply that the people hearing it must look to the Lord, depend on the Lord, and walk in the instruction of the Lord, not knowing how long it will be. Remember, that is the reason for the prophet, to get the people back into an active, obedient relationship with the Lord. That gives both the prophet and God credibility.

In the New Testament, Acts 11:28 records a prophecy Agabus gave to the people in Antioch:

> *"And one of them named Agabus stood up and foretold by the Spirit that there would be a great famine over all the world."*

The only way to know if Agabus's prophecy was true was to see if it actually happened. In this case, the people knew Agabus and his track record. They trusted him to speak for God and prepared ahead of time for the famine. It was true, and it did happen, giving him more credibility as a true prophet.

There were also false prophets, and people needed to know how to identify them. Therefore, God gave instructions to reveal them. One thing to watch for was presumption.

Presumption

Deuteronomy 18:22 says:

> When a prophet speaks in the name of the LORD, if the word does not come to pass or come true, that is a word that the LORD has not spoken; the prophet has spoken it presumptuously. You need not be afraid of him.

Old Testament prophecies brought with them judgment if they did not come to pass, which often caused fear among the people.

In this verse, Moses is describing the role of prophets who speak to the people on behalf of Yahweh—just as he had done. Rev. John Barry, a biblical scholar, writes the following in the *NIV Faithlife Study Bible*, a commentary application in the Logos Bible Study Platform: "The prophet was to be a mediator of divine revelation, reporting the words of Yahweh to the Israelite people. In the prophetic books, the prophets frequently preface their messages with formulas that identify their words as Yahweh's words, not their own. Prophets who presented their own words as if they were Yahweh's words would be subject to divine judgment."[4]

What exactly is presumption? Presumption is expressing something in a manner that is supposed to be true on the grounds of "probability." I notice how prophecy spoken in presumption often brings attention to the speaker more than to the Creator. In my own observations, I feel it can have a sense of arrogance and pride in its delivery, perhaps someone looking for a "pat on the back." Does that sound like God speaking?

Basically, presumption is stating an opinion as fact or, in this case, as God's words or opinion. It's assessing something and speaking what you believe God is saying about it as though He's saying it. It is usually based on a person's observation, not a revelation.

For instance, recall my personal anecdote from chapter one when I said my life group assessed my word and deemed it "false" or "off." This is exactly what happened. I spoke in presumption. I spoke what was on my heart and what I assessed, and I wanted to declare it as God's words to everyone. It was an immature, inexperienced, and foolish thing to do. I was not cautious. I was not well enough acquainted with my Master's voice or the Bible. I was young and liked feeling important. Thank God He has grace for us as we are learning. But no matter what our spiritual gift is, we must stay open to correction and even a rebuke.

It would be easy to conclude that identifying presumptions and false prophecies wouldn't be too difficult. After all, if it doesn't happen and it's not biblically sound, it must be false. We can get with that. If we know our Bible, we can rest assured. However, the situation may not be that cut and dried. We are left with a few other questions: What if a prophetic word is foretelling, and it doesn't happen in our lifetime? Or what if it's more cryptic, and we don't understand it, but then it happens later when revelation comes? What about dreams? What about visions? Can false prophecies come true? And the questions continue. I'll unfold the answer to these questions later in this book, but for now, let's grab that last one since there is some ambiguity among believers over it.

False Prophecy Appearing True

In Deuteronomy 13:1, Moses begins to warn the Israelites against being led astray by false prophets, friends, or family. He also explains what they should do about it. In this situation, he is concerned about the Israelites becoming idolatrous. However, the principle applies even in our times. Read Deuteronomy 13:1–5 to see what God shows Moses to do.

> *"If a prophet or a dreamer of dreams arises among you and gives you a sign or a wonder, and the sign or wonder that he tells you comes to pass, and if he says, 'Let us go after other gods,' which you have not known, 'and let us serve them,' you shall not listen to the words of that prophet or that dreamer of dreams. For the LORD your God is testing you, to know whether you love the LORD your God with all your heart and with all your soul. You shall walk after the LORD your God and fear Him and keep his commandments and obey his voice, and you shall serve Him and hold fast to Him. But that prophet or that dreamer of dreams shall be put to death, because he has taught rebellion against the LORD your God, who brought you out of the land of Egypt and redeemed you out of the house of slavery, to make you leave the way in which the LORD your God commanded you to walk. So you shall purge the evil from your midst."*

When we read this passage, we can already see that "prophetic" signs or wonders can come true, but the person giving the word can still be a false prophet. Take note that this spoken word is also referring to a "prediction." In such a case, how would we know the prophets are false?

The answer is because they steer us away from the one true God. They distract us from the covenant relationship that we have with and through Jesus. This passage puts great value on the content of what someone is teaching or proclaiming or dreaming. Did you catch the part where God is going to test us? God will test all prophets and prophecy.

Today, false prophets may not be so blatant and obvious with their proclamations to follow other gods. They may be much more subtle and deceptive, mixing plenty of truth with small amounts of deception. We have a very crafty adversary, and he goes crazy trying to deceive the church.

> *We have a very crafty adversary, and he goes crazy trying to deceive the church.*

I hope we are able to see the seriousness that goes with this spiritual gift and calling.

Read Deuteronomy 13:5 again:

"That prophet or dreamer shall be put to death because he has taught rebellion against the LORD your God."

And then God calls the words of the false prophet evil. The prophet is falsifying God's words to the people. He is lying, saying his words are from God! But in fact, he is spewing words from the evil one.

I've seen this scenario happen all too often in churches or on YouTube and TV today. A person gives a word out of emotionalism or for personal attention, or gives a word based on previously known information or presumption. There are plenty of reasons to list.

I hope we are taking this lesson to heart. These are people who are pretenders, attention seekers, self-proclaimed prophets, or those just speaking in "presumption." They are walking the edge of disaster and risking serious results with what they are doing. And yes, they will be judged harshly.

Last Look at Old Testament Examples

I've concluded the Old Testament prophets were taking the covenant promise made to the people and applying it relevantly to the people in their day. God used the prophets to help His people see themselves in the light of His covenant and see the consequences of their unbelief and rebellion. God was calling them to return to Him and be part of His promised restoration. The prophet's words were often accompanied by a foretelling of events that may or may not happen, depending on the response of the people.

It is worth noting that the words coming from the prophets of old were almost always in stark contrast to the perception of what the people thought they were doing and believing at the time. An example in Ezekiel's time was that the people didn't believe they would or even could be destroyed because God had made a covenant with them that included the land promised to them. They believed they were established forever. Any words of doom to them simply held no water. They determined the prophecies must be false.

But they were not false because the people were not following their own laws God's covenant had established. That covenant was strictly about worshiping the Lord your God and having no other gods before Him. Our God has no tolerance for other gods. He is a jealous God:

> *"For the LORD your God is a consuming fire, a jealous God."* (Deuteronomy 4:24)

CHAPTER 4

Qualifications of a Biblical Prophet

Is there any difference between Old Testament prophets and today's prophets or prophecy? The answer is both yes and no. Some things are the same, and other things have changed. Specifically, requirements or qualifications are on the list of changes.

God spoke through Jeremiah concerning an interesting qualification for one who speaks prophetically. Jeremiah writes this in Jeremiah 23:16–18:

> *Thus says the LORD of hosts: "Do not listen to the words of the prophets who prophesy to you, filling you with vain hopes. They speak visions of their own minds, not from the mouth of the LORD. They say continually to those who despise the word of the LORD, 'It shall be well with you'; and to everyone who stubbornly follows his own heart, they say, 'No disaster shall come upon you.'"*

For who among them has stood in the council of the LORD to see and to hear his word, or who has paid attention to his word and listened?

This passage includes an important signifier that marks a true Old Testament prophet. It is Jeremiah's admission to the divine council, where he received his mission and divine message. Note the divine council are not men, worldly leaders, or other prophets. They were not specially appointed people or judges, etc. They are members in God's heavenly hosts. They are a spiritual council created and appointed by God. Their purpose was to take part in the discussions God would have about decision-making. Psalm 82:1 tell us, "God has taken his place in the divine council; in the midst of the gods he holds judgment."

Another example of God conferring with his heavenly council is found in 1 Kings 22:19–21:

> And Micaiah said, "Therefore hear the word of the LORD: I saw the LORD sitting on his throne, and all the host of heaven standing beside Him on his right hand and on his left; and the LORD said, 'Who will entice Ahab, that he may go up and fall at Ramoth-gilead?' And one said one thing, and another said another. Then a spirit came forward and stood before the LORD, saying, 'I will entice him.'"

We read in this very scene that Micaiah the prophet was in the place of the heavenly hosts. John Barry writes in the *Faithlife Study Bible*, "The heavenly hosts refers to members of the heavenly court or the divine council who are allowed to discuss ways to carry out Yahweh's divine decree that Ahab must die."[1]

Jeremiah commented on the prophets in the Old Testament:

> For who among them has stood in the council of the LORD to see and to hear his word, or who has paid attention to his word and listened? (Jeremiah 23:18)

Have you been in the presence of the Lord God and His heavenly hosts? In Deuteronomy 18:18–20, God speaks to

Moses about how He wants to communicate to the people using appointed prophets. He says:

> "And I will put my words in his mouth, and he shall speak to them all that I command him. And whoever will not listen to my words that he shall speak in my name, I myself will require it of him. But the prophet who presumes to speak a word in my name that I have not commanded him to speak, or who speaks in the name of other gods, that same prophet shall die."

> *Have you been in the presence of the Lord God and His heavenly hosts?*

In the Old Testament, a message that a prophet speaks as though it's coming from God when it is not always leads to a misdirection where the people end up worshiping other gods in some form or fashion. The same is true of the New Testament prophets, but in many situations the result was much less obvious.

Before I give a specific example, we should pause, as this realization should make everyone desiring to prophesy cautious and careful. It is a heavy burden to walk in this office. It is a high-risk position. The prophet is held to the strictest of standards in relating the word of God to the people.

People mistakenly assumed that Simon Magus was using "the great power of God" in Acts 8:10 (NKJV). The people considered Simon to be the actual embodiment of God's Spirit. But he was false.

Later, in Acts 13:7–8, Paul came across Sergius Paulus at Paphos, another sorcerer who claimed to profess prophetic powers. Both men were leading people away from God to worship false gods.

Our Personality and the Holy Spirit

Is a prophet a mimicking parrot that repeats perfectly the words of the Most High? No. Dutch pastor and author Michael Willemse explains why in his article "Who Were the Old Testament Prophets?":

Each [prophet] brings the word of the LORD in a way consistent with their own education and experience; often showing interests and using examples consistent with their own background. Ezekiel, as a priest, shows a great familiarity with the temple and, indeed, much of his message has to do with the temple. Amos (a tree tender/sheep breeder), speaks of the Amorites *"tall as cedars and strong as oaks"* (2:9) and of Israel's survivors *"As a shepherd saves from the lion's mouth only two leg bones or an ear so will the Israelites be saved"* (3:12). God's word comes to His people through the personality of the prophet.[2]

We have established that a prophet is one who has received his mission from God by being in the presence of God and His divine council, and we can understand how the Spirit of God uses the personality (which may include the culture) of the person.

In a similar way we know that as a Christian, filled with the Holy Spirit, the Lord dwells in us as His temple. And in that place, He blends and works with us and through us, including in our personalities. He is not some foreign spirit possessing us or removing our minds or controlling our thoughts and bodies. He is a loving, intimate, kind, and caring Father and Creator who wants us to be just as He designed us. And He wants us in His originally designed kingdom as well.

A Servant Heart

Another qualification for a prophet and anyone who prophesies is having the heart of a servant. Isaiah 6:8–9 says:

> *And I heard the voice of the Lord saying, "Whom shall I send, and who will go for us?" Then I said, "Here I am! Send me." And he [the Lord] said, "Go, and say to this people ..."*

Notice how Isaiah volunteered for service when he heard the voice of the Lord.

Jeremiah was commissioned for service when God spoke to him, recorded in Jeremiah 1:4–5:

> *Now the word of the LORD came to me, saying, "Before I formed you in the womb I knew you, and before you were born I consecrated you; I appointed you a prophet to the nations."*

God created Jeremiah with a servant's heart from the womb.

We find one more example of a servant-heart prophet in Amos 7:14–15:

> *"I was no prophet, nor a prophet's son, but I was a herdsman and a dresser of sycamore figs. But the LORD took me from following the flock, and the LORD said to me, 'Go, prophesy to my people Israel.'"*

These are men serving as examples of being surrendered to His Majesty's service with a servant heart. The prophetic gift is inherently a call to service. We must realize that serving God is often connected to serving others. Throughout history, and even today, too many self-proclaimed prophets serve themselves for fame, money, or attention. Research these charlatans carefully by looking at their prophetic fulfillments, their self-proclamations, and whom they direct attention to, Jesus or themselves.

Another absolute qualification is one we already covered briefly: A prophet will not contradict the written Word of God. Just as in the Old Testament where the prophets were not to speak anything contrary to the covenant established by God, so it is with our Bible today. The New and Old Testaments are the only divinely inspired truths we have.

Let's be clear on this statement! No other books outside the Canon, historical or otherwise, can stand up to the measure of the prophetic words revealed by God to His people. You cannot measure the prophetic word against a non-inspired book. Non-inspired books may enhance understanding of the Bible, but they do not hold any ground for confirming prophetic-given words by anyone!

Other circumstantial qualifications have been cited as important but are given to specific situations. An example can be found in Numbers 12:5–8:

> And the LORD came down in a pillar of cloud and stood at the entrance of the tent and called Aaron and Miriam, and they both came forward. And he said, "Hear my words: If there is a prophet among you, I the LORD make myself known to him in a vision; I speak with him in a dream. Not so with my servant Moses. He is faithful in all my house. With him I speak mouth to mouth, clearly, and not in riddles, and he beholds the form of the LORD."

In this case, the Lord reveals His words and mission for them in dreams and visions, which really emphasizes the manner, or rather, the delivery more than a qualification.

Comparing the Old and New Testaments

Are the qualifications for the prophetic the same today as they were in the Old Testament? Joel speaks a word from the Lord that concerns our current day. However, this word for our current day started its revelation 2000 years ago when Christ came and ascended, imparting His Holy Spirit to us.

Joel 2:28–29 says:

"And it shall come to pass afterward, that I will pour out my Spirit on all flesh; your sons and your daughters shall prophesy, your old men shall dream dreams, and your young men shall see visions. Even on the male and female servants in those days I will pour out my Spirit."

Peter quotes this whole passage in Acts 2:17, and we are still seeing these words come to pass.

Dr. Michael S. Heiser makes the following comment about the book of Joel in the *Faithlife Study Bible*: "Joel reminds us that God is present and active in the world, working toward a difficult, but beautiful end—the restoration of peace and justice throughout the world."[3]

If God has poured out His Spirit on all, does this mean God has lifted all the qualifications and guidelines for giving prophecy or becoming a prophet? Does this mean anything goes if you believe in Jesus? And since God speaks to us directly, can we proclaim prophecy to everyone? Are we covered by God's grace if we proclaim prophetic words that are wrong? Will God's mercy cover us, and all will be just fine?

Well, not exactly. I will bring clarity to these questions as we continue.

Changes with the New Covenant

The Old Testament as a whole is a historical and prophetic record of events, declarations, and cryptic messages ultimately declaring the arrival of the Messiah. Many of them were cryptic at the time because they had to stay hidden until the day Christ came to earth so God's adversaries would have no idea of God's plan for man's redemption.

The beautiful thing about our day and age is that most of these prophecies have been revealed and fulfilled and now confirm the glorious plans of God's past, present, and future. When Jesus did come, He outsmarted the devil, died, and was resurrected so He could give us a new covenant. We read this in Matthew 5:17–18:

> Do not think that I have come to abolish the Law or the Prophets; I have not come to abolish them but to fulfill them. For truly, I say to you, until heaven and earth pass away, not an iota, not a dot, will pass from the Law until all is accomplished.

We can understand that Jesus did not say He came to replace the law and the prophets. He said He came to fulfill them. Rev. John Barry comments in the *Faithlife Study Bible*, "The Greek word for *fulfill* used here, *plēroō*, refers in this instance to carrying something out. Matthew is saying that Jesus performed or upheld that which was required by the law and met the expectations of the predictions about Him in the writings of the prophets. In Him, the Law and the Prophets reached their fullest expression."[4]

Matthew 5:19 supports this idea:

Therefore whoever relaxes one of the least of these commandments and teaches others to do the same will be called least in the kingdom of heaven, but whoever does them and teaches them will be called great in the kingdom of heaven.

The law is written in our hearts and minds, and Jesus did not abolish that but revealed understanding through His death, resurrection, and impartation of the Holy Spirit.

Hebrews 10:16 says:

"This is the covenant that I will make with them after those days, declares the Lord: I will put my laws on their hearts, and write them on their minds."

Jesus did not do away with the law or the prophetic or the prophets; however, some things will change with how the prophetic is expressed.

The Old Testament was an era of covenant law and judgment. A prophet's primary function in the Old Testament was to serve as God's representative or ambassador by communicating God's word to His people. Prophets never spoke on their own authority or shared their personal opinions, but rather delivered the message God Himself gave them. That foundational understanding does not change in the New Testament era.

Peter supports this in 2 Peter 1:20–21:

Knowing this first of all, that no prophecy of Scripture comes from someone's own interpretation. For no prophecy was ever produced by the will of man, but men spoke from God as they were carried along by the Holy Spirit.

With our Lord Jesus on the scene, the most prominent prophetic voice in the New Testament is clearly Jesus Himself. Another prophetic voice with Him was John the Baptist. Luke clarified this in Luke 1:76–79:

> "And you, child, will be called the prophet of the Most High; for you will go before the Lord to prepare his ways, to give knowledge of salvation to his people in the forgiveness of their sins, because of the tender mercy of our God, whereby the sunrise shall visit us from on high to give light to those who sit in darkness and in the shadow of death, to guide our feet into the way of peace."

Unveiling His New Covenant

With the unveiling of the new covenant, we can begin to see changes that come with understanding the prophetic word and how it's used. Hebrews 8:10, 12 states:

> "For this is the covenant that I will make with the house of Israel after those days, declares the Lord: I will put my laws into their minds, and write them on their hearts, and I will be their God, and they shall be my people ... For I will be merciful toward their iniquities, and I will remember their sins no more."

In Luke 22:20, Jesus states His imminent death enacts the new covenant centered on forgiveness: *"This cup that is poured out for you is the new covenant in my blood."*

Hebrews 12:24 calls Jesus "the mediator of a new covenant." Paul writes in 2 Corinthians 3:5–6:

> *Our sufficiency is from God, who has made us sufficient to be ministers of a new covenant, not of the letter but of the Spirit.*

These verses change some things that pertain to the gifts of prophecy and the office of a prophet.

For some, it's a point of contention and argument. Some still try to hold to the Old Testament system and believe that grace takes a back seat to the law. It is a discussion worth digging into for the freedom of expressing what God wants to communicate.

CHAPTER 5

Maturing Prophetically

The Visitation

As a young Christian man, seeking God was a full-time commitment in my mind. I made a point of reading the Word, praying, and desiring to have some kind of spiritual encounter that would strengthen my commitment.

I believe the Lord was listening and agreed something would be needed to "lock me in" for the long haul of my Christian walk. Although I could share many experiences and encounters, I've chosen to share two specific ones because of the significance they had on me.

The first life-altering experience happened while I was living at Lake Tahoe when I was in my late twenties. I had two roommates, Chris and Jim. They had their own bedrooms, but we shared a common living space and a kitchen in an apartment-style condo that was on the second floor of the building. Our rear balcony looked out into a forest. The front door went out to a long second-floor balcony that had a staircase at each end.

During these days, I was still new in my faith and seeking God for a closer relationship. On this particular morning, it was 5:00 a.m. when I glanced at the digital clock. The sun was not quite up. As I sat up in bed, I heard noise coming from the dining area in our apartment. My bedroom door was ajar, and my blurry vision could see some commotion. I got up to see what it was.

I opened my door and saw Jesus sitting at the dining table. I wasn't sure what to think. Chris and Jim were also sitting there, so I came in and sat down. They were asking Him questions but were not understanding His answers and were getting frustrated. I felt compassion for Jesus, so I finally said, "Stop it—just leave Him alone. You're not asking Him the right questions." My roommates just stared at me.

So, I asked Jesus a simple question: "Can we see heaven?" His penetrating eyes looked into me, and He said, "No." He continued to look into me with a fixed gaze. And suddenly, I understood. Then I said, "Can we feel heaven?" He smiled and said, "Yes!" I had changed my question to mean it in a spiritual sense.

> So, I asked Jesus a simple question: "Can we see heaven?" His penetrating eyes looked into me, and He said, "No."

At this point, noise was increasing as if others were trying to get His attention, and all I wanted to do was protect Him and stop the clamoring. I stood up, and then He stood up. He looked at me and then told me to come closer. As I did, He stepped behind me. My arms were crossed over my chest. He put his arms around me, grabbed my opposite hands, and pulled me inside of Him. We suddenly became one. I took a deep breath, and He was beside me again.

Then He turned and said, "It's time for Me to go." I didn't want Him to leave. I followed Him, thinking I would just go with Him. I went with Him out the front door, but He moved too quickly for me. It wasn't like speed, but rather like a dimensional shift.

Suddenly, He was on the ground level walking away. From the balcony level above, I shouted, "Stop! Wait!" I realized I was not going to be able to go with Him. He just stopped and turned to look at me. Not really knowing what to say, I simply said, "I love You!" And like someone who says something in exact synchronicity, He said "I love you" back to me.

Moments later, I woke up in my bed asking myself what had just happened. The clock read 5:30 a.m.

This encounter has been with me for over forty years, and any time I wanted to doubt His existence, this immutable memory makes it simply impossible. I relate to this event as a visitation from the Spirit of the Lord that locked me into my faith. It has kept a fire burning in my soul to pursue what and how life in Christ is supposed to be. This event also signified the initial point of a spiritual infusion of the prophetic gift in my life.

Living by Faith

The second event that changed my perception of my destiny as a follower of Jesus came soon after.

This dream started out with me being chased by some very ugly men (picture a gnarly, angry, Charles Manson-like group). They were chasing me on foot and catching up quickly. I turned to look back at them, and somehow they had found an old van, like a 1960s-style, beat-up Ford, and were driving after me.

It was obvious I could not outrun them. It was clear to me they were definitely going to catch up to me and run me down to kill me. Then something came over me, and I decided I couldn't outrun them, so I chose to face them head-on. I stopped, put out my hand in front of me, and braced myself for the impact.

The van went right through me ... or should I say, I went right through the van! It was like a phantom van of evil.

When I turned around to look at it, I realized they weren't going to give up and had turned the van around to come after me again.

Having withstood the first phantom impact, I now felt empowered. I started running as fast as I could along this dirt road through a forest. I could hear and feel the van getting very, very close, so I opened up my arms, pushed off the ground, and began to fly.

I soared higher and higher up over the treetops of the forest below. It was very exciting, and I began to test what I could do with flight, which wasn't much. I told myself to hold steady.

Eventually, having no control over my ability, I began to lose altitude, and the drop began to accelerate. I was worried I would hit the treetops because I was getting closer and closer. In the near distance, I saw a lake and figured if I could just make it there, I'd be okay. Holding onto my flight with intense concentration and praying for God to help me, I cleared the treetops and then dropped like a rock into the water. I sank straight to the bottom of the lake.

I opened my eyes under the water and saw in front of me an enormous book being opened for me. When I looked to see what was written, I saw FAITH! written across both pages in big black letters. Then I heard a voice say to me, "You shall live by faith." Then I woke up.

I was certainly shaken and curious about the entire dream. It was incredibly realistic. Looking back, I am able to see much more meaning than I could at the time, such as the van of men representing demonic figures trying to stop me or scare me. The flight represented a span of time to test, learn, and trust Jesus, and then the surrender to living a life of faith.

So, why have I included these two events from my life when we are looking at the gifts and calling of prophecy? Because it takes an enormous commitment to face the demons in your life that are trying to chase you down and stop you, and it takes a great deal of commitment and stepping out in faith to grow and mature in your spiritual gift.

As one called to the office or gift of the prophetic, your faith becomes incredibly intertwined with the Holy Spirit in the sense that a blending of His power begins to unveil through you. This kind of revelation of faith begins to change your perceptions. You begin to realize that faith in the Father is infinite. It is without time, space, depth, or even full comprehension. It is infinite just as our God is infinite. The same understanding of His mercy and love becomes evident, and your heart, mind, and even your physical abilities take on new depth and profound significance.

King David, or shall I say Prophet David, is so good at communicating this idea in his psalms. Encountering God and being in His presence is essential for all who think they are called to be prophetic or a prophet.

Now don't misunderstand me. None of this limits God from using anyone prophetically. He can use anyone, anytime, in any circumstance. And it's not even limited to Christians! They don't have to fit the "criteria." But entering into a sacred space, an intimate space regarding relationship, is something that seems to be recognizable in biblical prophetic people, both in the Bible and in the church today.

My Gift Takes Shape

In the first chapter, I left off when I was attending an evening life group and had just given an "unapproved" word critiqued by my trusted, more mature brothers and sisters. One important thing I learned from that situation is that I never wanted to feel that embarrassment again. I needed to refocus, study, read, and pray a lot. A whole lot.

I came to the realization that hearing the Shepherd's voice (Jesus's) is the most important thing to nurture my spiritual gift.

My ability to distinguish His voice needed to improve. It really didn't matter that I was beginning to see things in the Spirit that were significant in some regard to my prayers. If I didn't recognize my Master's voice, those visions could be completely misunderstood, misrepresented even, misused, and possibly abused. For the next couple years, I continued receiving visual insights, which became even more accessible and available to my thoughts. I spent far more time seeking and a great deal more quiet time in the presence of God, learning, listening, and practicing to hear His voice.

How does one practice hearing His voice? This can be learned several ways. The way I chose was to write down whatever I believed God was saying to me, and then submit it to my close and trusted friends like my pastor, Eric, as well as one or two others. They could give me feedback or explain to me what was biblically accurate and what might be difficult to consider. It wasn't as dramatic as it might seem. And really, it wasn't much of a big deal. Mostly, they just helped me with the biblical side because they had a much stronger knowledge of the Bible than I did at the time. I believed I could trust them.

I also asked more mature brothers to pray separately from me and write what God spoke to them. Then we would gather together and compare notes. Quite often we would get confirmation from each other, which built up our faith.

Eventually, I did become quite acquainted with and could be confident in that familiar voice that would come in my quiet times. I can't express the importance of this because our adversary will try to imitate the Master's voice. Therefore, we must know every nuance of how He speaks to each of us. The reading of His Word reinforces His voice in our hearts and minds.

As I matured, the wisdom in my gift grew, and eventually, the leadership in my church believed in the ability of my gift and felt comfortable with me expressing it in certain public situations.

What were those situations, you might ask? I believe different kinds of leaders have different beliefs and understandings of how prophetic gifts works. Throughout the book, I'll be giving examples and discussing the prophetic person's responsibilities and responses. Nevertheless, church leaders have to talk about and maybe teach about the prophetic so the church can experience the freedom to express, protect, and develop it. I believe in accountability with all the spiritual gifts by those who understand them.

Personally, I want no pride, arrogance, or personal identity to be derived from my gift. My identity must be fully grounded in my relationship with my Father, the Most High, because of who I am in His family. If that sometimes means limiting my gift or holding it back until a leader is receptive, then so be it. After all, it's God's gift! Not mine. He gets to choose the place, time, and manner in which He wants to use it, including how, where, when, and how much it gets to be expressed. He is in control, especially in the circumstances surrounding me at the time.

If I don't get to express it, I have two more options. I can express it anyway and risk being disruptive, causing frustration, and possibly confusion, with the leadership. Or I can leave that place, and then I have no opportunity to use my gift for God until I "hopefully" find somewhere I will be accepted.

No matter what, I can press in and ask God what He wants to do about it. I have experienced several options. When faced with absolute rejection of the gifts of the Holy Spirit, a third option always worked best and honestly resulted in an open comfortable expression. The third option was to start or get involved in a home group that allowed the gifts of the Spirit to be expressed and grow. However, even in those settings, a safe environment, just like the one Pastor Eric provided for me in the new expressions of my visions, was important.

In the church I attended at that time, I was invited to be on the prayer team that would pray for people at the end of the service at the front of the church. It was here I developed a public exercise of my gift. Usually what happened was someone would approach me for prayer, and I would get an image in my mind about the person. I would then speak what that image was, and they would usually confirm to me if that meant something to them. If it didn't, I would simply pray, but the prayers seemed to regularly unveil a mystery or an unexpected revelation that brought healing, direction, comfort, encouragement, and, on some occasions, repentance.

Did I ever expose someone's sin? NEVER! Did I ever see it with my spiritual eyes? Definitely. But GOD IS NOT A GOSSIP! Our God is a loving gentleman who cares so much for us that He chooses not to humiliate but rather to bring conviction, repentance, and healing. God did give me instructions at times to talk with someone privately and explore carefully and gently if they were willing to confess their sin, but that was rare. When it did happen, it was with other leadership present, and never was it done with pressure or judgment. God brings the conviction, not us.

Over the next year or more, I began to become much more acquainted with the presence and Spirit of the Lord. I would have intimate conversations that would always lead me to ask for more revelation and understanding of people, situations, and circumstances, including for myself! I wanted to increase in wisdom as to how to use my gift to its fullest.

I began to learn the nuances of the prophetic. Oh yes, it does have nuances, much like a musical instrument can be played and expressed in many different ways. If you think about it, prophets must be sensitive to timing, tone, like soft, loud, firm, or gentle, and purpose. They must also think about whether a word is meant to be public or to private, determining if it's for themselves personally, for someone else individually, or for a group of people.

I have given a public word at times not knowing whom it was for and then later realizing it was, in fact, for myself. Even recently I had a succession of dreams I shared with a close friend, thinking it must be some cryptic message for the church. But he unveiled the meaning to me, helping me realize the dreams were meant for me personally, and in fact, helped me to grow spiritually.

That's why accountability with your gift is important. Accountability really means submitting. Submitting what you believe you are receiving from God to a trusted brother or sister in Jesus. Often our own perspective on what we get from God is incomplete or challenged by our circumstances and misinterpretations.

We must remember that God is a communicator. And He doesn't only speak in one tone, one cadence, or one level. Sometimes, He chooses to speak in a symbolic or cryptic manner. In those times, we need others to help and pray with us for discernment, understanding, and interpretation. We are vessels for the Holy Spirit, but we have a responsibility to use wisdom with the Lord's revelations. Remember, He is using our personalities to communicate His words or actions. Isn't that amazing?

CHAPTER 6

Experiences and Foundations

I want to re-emphasize how fortunate we are in our day and age to have the Bible. It is the testimony of God to the authority of His own Word. God's Word is an infallible guide to understand a personal relationship with Him regarding the past, present, and future. As I've said before, the Bible's infallibility means that we can hold any word of prophecy up to the Bible and be sure if it is true or false.

Following is a quick recap on what to check when you hear someone speak prophetically. Ask these seven questions and do a little analysis:

Is the word in line with God's character as the Bible describes Him?

Is it in line with the principles of salvation?

Does it line up with Scripture kept in context?

Is it in line with the desires expressed by God for His church?

Does it bring edification, consolation, exhortation, and/or revelation?

Does it bring rebuke, correction, and/or knowledge of the future?

Does it give direction producing results that glorify Jesus, the Father, and the Holy Spirit?

As you can see, for us to judge prophecy or words spoken by people in authority, we need to read the Bible as much as possible and use it as our plumb line.

The Holy Spirit Moves

In the late 1960s, the charismatic movement in churches in the United States began to express the gifts of the Holy Spirit in new dynamic ways during church services. By the 1980s, church denominations, such as Vineyard, were formed specifically for the public expression of gifts like healing, speaking in tongues, words of knowledge, and prophetic proclamations.

Obviously, plenty of controversy happened between the traditional church and the rising charismatic ones. Some churches split, and some congregations were confused, primarily due to lack of knowledge and education. People took sides, and to this day, you will find churches labeled conservative or Renewalists, also called charismatic. But is it really something new? What did the charismatic churches of the '60s and '80s experience and why?

Throughout history, moves or expressions of the Holy Spirit have occurred in churches, groups, cities, and towns. We have usually called them revivals. If the charismatic movement was a revival of sorts, what did the movement revive? The simplest answer is found in 1 Corinthians 12:4–11 regarding Paul's words about the gifts of the Spirit.

I'm not going to get into the doctrinal conflicts and controversy about this, but I am going to focus on one perspective. We want to be biblical Christians that live, walk, and serve as God intended from the beginning of creation until He fulfills His purposes with the new earth.

The question is, how do we do that? Throughout Scripture, the church is taught, encouraged, and even commanded to live out the expression of the gifts of the Spirit so the Gospel can be preached effectively and with power. Those spiritual gifts come just as the text indicates ... spiritually. So, who activates those gifts? According to Jesus, He does, by the infilling of His Spirit.

Luke writes this in Acts 1:8:

"But you will receive power when the Holy Spirit has come upon you, and you will be my witnesses in Jerusalem and in all Judea and Samaria, and to the end of the earth."

The first church I attended was heavily focused on teaching the scriptures and giving biblical life lessons. The second church I was a part of was focused more on the experiences and expressions of the spiritual gifts. Both of them had their purpose, and both were used to bring people to Jesus and lay a foundation for a relationship with Him.

For some reason, in those days, it was uncommon to find a church strong in emphasizing both. But I believe over time, those churches did grow in both ways to some degree.

Eventually, a challenge began to show up for leaders who were encouraging the gifts like public speaking in tongues, public prophecy, and words of knowledge. The challenge was confusion and, dare I say, a bit of chaos during services. Distractions and frustrations became evident.

I was witness to all of it firsthand: the power, the excitement, the dynamics, the healing, the revival, the frustration, the misdirection, the confusion, the misunderstanding, the lack of order and clarity, and, in some situations, the lies and false prophetic proclamations.

So, what went wrong, and what did they do? Sadly, a great number of churches simply stopped allowing the expressions of the Holy Spirit to manifest publicly. They just didn't know what to do, so they took the easy way out. What followed was dwindling congregations, less outreach, if any, and exclusivity. As a result, many conservative churches like these pointed their fingers in blame at the charismatic ones.

> *Sadly, a great number of churches simply stopped allowing the expressions of the Holy Spirit to manifest publicly.*

In Ecclesiastes 1:9, Solomon says there's nothing new under the sun. Even in the day of the twelve apostles, similar things were going on. Why? Where are all the peace-loving, harmonized believers that live, learn, and grow together as one in the Spirit and are of the same mind, sharing everything for the good of the church? It kind of sounds like a utopia, doesn't it?

The Charismatic Challenge

We are contending with two major issues, the sin nature of mankind and the activity of an adversary who wants to corrupt God's plans and stay actively present.

Consider some of the obvious things of human nature, or sin nature, that can interfere with God's plan. Some examples are the desire for public attention or feeling important, being emotionally involved, or speaking from emotionalism. Other issues are a lack of understanding of the spiritual gifts that leads to their misuse, overactive imaginations that may not be submitted to the Holy Spirit, personal agendas, a desire to cause disruption for the sake of excitement, or an emphasis on the "entertainment."

I'm sure you can think of more humanistic, human nature-based reasons for frustration among church leadership. Add to those the adversarial involvement. Oh, let me guess, you think there isn't any in church, right? Because we're all Christians? Personally, I think churches are where the adversaries love to hang out until they are discovered and expelled. These enemies love to cause as much chaos as possible where humans give them access to take advantage of any situation they can.

I've seen demonic manifestations right in the middle of a service. I've seen demonic influence try to convince a large crowd to follow nonbiblical principles preached by a wayward soul who pretends to be righteous but uses New Age ideas from his so-called revelation. We have to be so careful when preachers introduce ideas, social behaviors, and cultural justifications for the sake of their own popularity. It is something relatively prevalent in our American churches today.

CHAPTER 7

Public Prophecies in the Church

What's a Church to Do?

How can a church, especially one over the size of a dozen, manage and deal with all the variations of humanistic, human nature-based interactions regarding the spiritual gifts? Again, most take the easy way out and say, "We believe in them, but we don't practice or allow them in our church."

Does that seem a bit odd to you? What if I said that I believe we are commanded to share the Gospel, but we don't because it causes too much conflict? You might look at me sideways. How will people hear the Gospel?

When I was a missionary in China, if we shared the Gospel, we went to jail. Some people might believe in that case it's understandable we would keep our mouths shut. Oh really? Is that what Jesus said? Is that what the disciples and apostles did? By no means. Consequences are always going to be there, so you have to face and deal with them.

Let's put our focus back on prophecy and speaking a word God gives to someone. And let's use the example of being in a congregation or group of people. Let's say someone reveals a prophetic word or a word of knowledge to the group openly. There are plenty of variables to consider.

Do you think we have to consider who's in that group? Some people would say no, it makes no difference because if God's speaking, then that's His concern. I was in this example, and I personally know people who were spiritually injured because they were not mature enough to realize what was happening. A spiritual injury can happen when a person, due to existing sensitivities, cannot comprehend or process a personal or situational revelation at that time. Their perception may be skewed for whatever reason. This can lead them to turn away, or even turn against God. This type of situation really concerns the delivery of the prophecy, not the prophetic word itself. The word itself may be 100 percent accurate.

> *If God gives me a word or a vision, it's my responsibility to assess my surroundings and my circumstances before giving that word.*

Remember when I said God uses our personalities, our hearts, and our minds with His Spirit? Part of that is Him trusting us with the wisdom of knowing our situations and our potential impact. And that's when the nuances come into play. If God gives me a word or a vision, it's my responsibility to assess my surroundings and my circumstances before giving that word. I need to consider where I am, whom I'm with, and how God wants me to speak. God is a gentleman, a loving Father as much as He is a warrior. He can desire a firm, strong delivery or a gentle, loving one. We are made in His image and have beautiful intonations and tones with our voices. We also have the ability to discern the right timing. We really just have to pay closer attention to our guide, the Holy Spirit, and what He wants us to observe before we speak.

An Old Testament example of this is Ezekiel. He was a temple priest living in Babylon. He was surrounded by false prophets, idol worship, and a ridiculous amount of sexual perversion. These sins were all happening among God's people, who believed they could worship Yahweh alongside their perversions. In his prophetic language, Ezekiel uses temple symbols, even from the Babylonian temples. He describes angelic creatures that were used in Egyptian art, and he uses the language of the people he's about to speak to, write to, and act out in front of. Dr. Michael Heiser discusses the entire cultural background, including the language used in Babylon during Ezekiel's time, in his podcast series on the book of Ezekiel.[1]

In other words, Ezekiel first observed his surroundings, then assessed what was going on, considered the people's condition, and finally addressed his message from God accordingly and in obedience to how God wanted it delivered. Some of his messages had gaps of time or changes in location. In others, Ezekiel needed to figure out basic elements for how to perform the task God was asking. One example in Ezekiel 8:7–13 was when God impressed on him to dig a hole through a wall to leave with his backpack, as a symbol of Yahweh leaving the temple. Ezekiel had to decide what wall, where, when, and how. God trusted Ezekiel to use his wisdom and his observation to follow through with the demonstration and act out the proclamation. Ezekiel grabbed a few clothes, likely went to the back wall of his house, and, with his hands, knocked a hole in the wall to crawl through while people watched him and probably scratched their heads, thinking he was a crazy prophet.

The point is that if God is trusting you to be His voice and to share His message for someone or a group, He also trusts you to know how to deliver it.

Let's get back to our local church and what's going to happen in a congregation when a word from God comes forth through an individual. Whether we know the individual or not, we have to decide what to do. Do we automatically trust and believe their word? What if their words are untrue or do not line up with the Bible? We can't put them to death like the Old Testament laws commanded.

Order in the Church

The Apostle Paul encountered the frustrations of disorder concerning the expression of spiritual gifts in the church. And he was kind enough to teach us by his revelatory wisdom what to do. We read his instructions in 1 Corinthians 14:26–33:

> *What then, brothers? When you come together, each one has a hymn, a lesson, a revelation, a tongue, or an interpretation. Let all things be done for building up. If any speak in a tongue, let there be only two or at most three, and each in turn, and let someone interpret. But if there is no one to interpret, let each of them keep silent in church and speak to himself and to God. Let two or three prophets speak, and let the others weigh what is said. If a revelation is made to another sitting there, let the first be silent. For you can all prophesy one by one, so that all may learn and all be encouraged, and the spirits of prophets are subject to prophets. For God is not a God of confusion but of peace.*

Paul is giving us instructions revealed by God here. And for the sake of the prophets or prophetic people, let's focus on verses 29–33. I'm sure we can agree Paul is suggesting that two or three prophets should not all speak at the same time over each other. Neither is he saying that after one speaks, it's okay to argue with another speaking a different version of the message. That's pretty obvious and petty. But what he is doing is suggesting a limit as to how much is proclaimed.

Why would he do that? What right does he have to suggest that? Paul knows something we don't. Paul understands something about the Holy Spirit and the way He communicates that we need to listen to. Paul is explaining the peacefulness and order the Holy Spirit desires when people express spiritual gifts.

Prophetic Checks and Balances

Paul says let the others weigh what is said. Who are "the others"? In that culture and history, it was accepted and expected that older prophets were to train up younger ones. An example of this is Eli training up young Samuel in 1 Samuel. That tradition and practice carried through the Old Testament, the Second Temple (between the testaments), and the New Testament eras. And if anyone was familiar with that practice, it was definitely Paul.

It's important to understand the intent of these verses by using the Greek definitions. In this case the Greek word for "other" is *allos*, with a couple choices in its interpretation. In the context here as it relates to the rest of the section referring to people speaking in tongues and God's order, this word is best interpreted as "another." This would refer to other prophets, such as older, more experienced ones weighing in on the word spoken.

What does it mean to "weigh in" on the word? The book of 1 John helps us with that one.

> Beloved, do not believe every spirit, but test the spirits to see whether they are from God, for many false prophets have gone out into the world. (1 John 4:1).

John also explains how testing spirits works in 1 John 4:2–3:

> By this you know the Spirit of God: every spirit that confesses that Jesus Christ has come in the flesh is from God, and every spirit that does not confess Jesus is not from God. This is the spirit of the antichrist, which you heard was coming and now is in the world already.

The first step to weighing a word is considering who is giving it. We need to find out if the person speaking the prophetic word is a confessed believer who is trusted with the Word.

How are we to weigh the prophetic word? The Greek word for "weigh" here is *diakrino*, meaning to separate thoroughly, discern, discriminate, and decide.[2] Weighing a word is not necessarily the same as judging it. It is a gentler term. In other words, it is not harsh, like a stern rebuke, if the word is off. But it still suggests correction. For example, correcting your children for the sake of learning is gentler than abruptly or even harshly stopping them from continuing in their trajectory.

Paul continues in 1 Corinthians 14:30 (NKJV):

> But if anything is revealed to another who sits by, let the first keep silent.

The word "another," again, is a reference to other prophets. This is further clarified in 1 Thessalonians 5:20–21:

> *Do not despise prophecies, but test everything; hold fast what is good.*

In other words, this is not about whose word is bigger, better, or stronger; it is a respectful and honorable recognition that God is speaking through an individual for a specific purpose, and He may be using more than one person to get His point across.

Paul continues with a glimpse into the primary purpose of public prophecy in a church body.

We continue with verse 31:

> *For you can all prophesy one by one, so that all may learn and all may be encouraged.*

This describes the purpose, "to learn and be encouraged." Can correction be encouraging? Yes, when the communication is done in wisdom. Correction is not criticism. If the desire is there to improve, grow in character, and learn, then correction will connect to that person's aspirations, resulting in encouragement.

Paul continues in verse 32:

> *And the spirit of the prophets are subject to the prophets.*

This verse brings more support to "other" meaning "another" in verse 29.

Therefore, it is pretty clear that when prophecies are spoken, they ought to be in the presence of others with the same gift and given with the understanding that the word is subject to the others for affirmation, confirmation, or maybe correction.

Finally, in verses 33 and 37–40, Paul puts a cap on the

discussion for people who are still wanting to ignore the suggestion:

> For God is not a God of confusion but of peace ... If anyone thinks that he is a prophet, or spiritual, he should acknowledge that the things I am writing to you are a command of the Lord. If anyone does not recognize this, he is not recognized. So, my brothers, earnestly desire to prophesy, and do not forbid speaking in tongues. But all things should be done decently and in order.

Facing Difficult Circumstances

After having many discussions with brothers well versed in the Word and operating in these gifts, I've come to some understanding that people who claim to have the call of prophet or who give prophetic words may be in a place where other prophetic people are absent. In these situations, we are accountable to leadership that understands the office or the gift might consider stopping the word from being spoken for any number of revelatory reasons, such as inappropriate timing, expressing in the wrong tone, such as frustration or even anger, or coming from the human spirit and not the Holy Spirit.

This can be really difficult for the person with the gift to accept. Imagine if you're a great cook, and someone comes along and says the way you're cooking isn't the way they understand cooking. So, you need to change it or to change the recipe. Or just stop cooking! You might think that's ridiculous! You cook the way you were taught or how you understand cooking from education and experience. Why would you listen?

The difference is when you're cooking for a restaurant, especially a very high-end restaurant, you have a boss. And that boss gets to call the shots, whether you like it or not. And you have a choice. You might just leave. When it comes to the prophetic ministry, whatever you choose to do about the difference of perspective with leadership, use wisdom more than emotions. So be careful, because your choice might have negative results for you or for the mission God has for you.

This scenario is about submitting to others in authority with or without the gift. In a public setting, it prevents embarrassment or problems of confusion in a church where the prophets or the ones giving a prophecy have an understanding with each other of accountability and respect. We must be honest about one thing—some people really struggle to submit to authority. A mature prophet will show true humility and gladly receive correction if it is explained. That is a responsibility of the person in authority. This is not an invitation for personal comments or opinion. The correction is to be done by true revelation from the Spirit of God or biblical clarification.

If a public prophecy seems odd, isn't easily understood, or maybe is just uncomfortable or without clear revelation, sometimes it's best for others (including other prophets) to remain silent so as not to discourage or stop the gift that may, in fact, be from the Lord. The word can be weighed in discussion afterward.

This understanding falls in line with 1 Corinthians 14:32 requiring the spirits (defined as the mental disposition of the human soul) of the prophets to be in subjection to other prophets. It is a laying down of human pride.

Simply put, there should be an understanding between those called as prophets and the leadership of the body to be submitted to each other for correction. Again, not criticism! This requires love and vulnerability and will prevent confusion, as written in verse 33: *"God is not a God of confusion but of peace."*

Why are all these "checks and balances" necessary? Read 1 Corinthians 13:9–13 (NKJV):

> *For we know in part and we prophesy in part. But when that which is perfect has come, then that which is in part will be done away. When I was a child, I spoke as a child, I understood as a child, I thought as a child; but when I became a man, I put away childish things. For now we see in a mirror, dimly, but then face to face. Now I know in part, but then I shall know just as I also am known. And now abide faith, hope, love, these three; but the greatest of these is love.*

Note the context of this verse is still regarding the gifts of the Spirit.

We are dependent on God's mercy and grace as we do our best to grow up in His Spirit, practicing in faith, hope, and love the gifts which He has so graciously bestowed. It should be our desire to become spiritually mature; but as in every aspect of life, we must stay open to learning, correction, and the sharpening of our spiritual senses by allowing others to speak into our lives. This is part of equipping the saints.

With these things in mind, we can understand the principles of 1 Corinthians 13 and 14 needing to surround all that we do and practice.

CHAPTER 8

Experiencing Prophecy

We've done a good amount of exploring the prophetic gift and how it gets expressed today. But what about the gift itself? Is there more to it?

My gifts grew as I pursued the Spirit of the Lord. The more I sought understanding and grew in both biblical education and experiential involvement, the more my personality and character shifted and changed. And to be very honest, age does have its effects on our perceptions and natural behavior toward and about certain subjects and views. It is a good thing to seek after God, wanting to know and understand just how He sees and involves people. After years of learning about the gift, I have seen that humility is one of the most important traits of exercising the gift as God intended. It often seems like humility is elusive, but it is a very important characteristic we must pursue. Of course, as soon as you think you're being humble, you're not.

Nevertheless, humility has to stay as our number one focus if we want to grow in the gift of the prophetic. This is not a humanly natural response, as I understand. I'm talking about being humble with a gift that draws attention.

> *Humility has to stay as our number one focus if we want to grow in the gift of the prophetic.*

Therefore, what is one of the ways humility is learned?

The answer is submission and accountability. It is simply a healthy practice that God requires from us. Consider James 4:5–8, 10:

> *Or do you suppose it is to no purpose that the Scripture says, "He yearns jealously over the spirit that He has made to dwell in us"? But He gives more grace. Therefore it says, "God opposes the proud but gives grace to the humble." Submit yourselves therefore to God. Resist the devil, and he will flee from you. Draw near to God, and He will draw near to you. Cleanse your hands, you sinners, and purify your hearts, you double-minded ... Humble yourselves before the Lord, and he will exalt you.*

A New Level and Responsibility

In my life, a transition began to take place the more I practiced my gift of hearing the Spirit of the Lord while praying for others. It took about ten to fifteen years of refining my gift through heightening my sensitivity to His voice and the nuances of the Spirit. I began getting more information, detailed information about current circumstances both in people's lives and in our local church. The information I was getting was not usually known. I was getting input from God from His perspective. They were usually insights concerning direction and the spiritual health of the people as a group—hidden information for the purpose of prayer.

The only way I know how to explain it is that my eyes were being opened to the good and to that which was a concern to the Lord directly. Now, this was like experiencing a new level of responsibility. I was needing wisdom regarding what and how to deal with the revelations that were concerning, especially when it came to the leadership of a church. This was really a test for me.

This proper application of the gift in challenging circumstances was learned through trial and error. To begin with, when a revelation or a word comes in the form of correction to a situation or circumstance involving church leadership or church health, you don't just give the word and walk away. Remember, we are not living under the same covenant laws of the Old Testament. We have a new covenant of grace, mercy, love, peace, and repentance.

It is important to address the proper procedure when giving a prophetic word to a church or church leadership. I have been present and witnessed when a corrective prophetic word came forth publicly in a church service that was proclaimed without consideration of the situation. Let me just say—it's ugly, hurtful, confusing, usually unclear, and typically not done in a loving, merciful, and gracious spirit. That said, the desired results, as can be expected, often fail. This may seem obvious. However, allow me to put some details and an example around this situation.

My experience comes from a church walking in the Spirit. The church allowed the practice of the spiritual gifts and was set up for validating the public giving of a word. This example comes from a spiritually mature staff and leadership who were experienced teachers, preachers, and believers.

In this example, the problem arose when the congregation was confronted with several issues at once. It was a larger congregation and, therefore, diverse in many ways. First, there were new believers who have no clue what was going on. Second, there were members who were oblivious to why this word of correction was given when they hadn't seen anything regarding it. Finally, there was simply the condition of the human heart and whether it was prepared to accept it or not. If you want to start an argument or a fight, this is a good start. (Obviously these things are not exclusive to a public prophetic word.)

Please realize that the word may be 100 percent accurate, purely from God, and absolutely necessary! But the manner of delivery is of the utmost importance. God trusts the giver of His word to be His servant and to be responsible, but the truth is we are human, we make mistakes, and we don't always do what we are told or pay attention to the details.

In all honesty, so often as prophetic people, we get a word from God, and it makes our heart race and our minds go. Excitement ensues. We just jump into it and blurt out what's moving through us. Sometimes it's a real rush in our bodies and minds. It can also be like a furnace burning inside us, ready to release. So, the prophetic individual needs to develop the discipline of delivery.

I feel like I need to make a quick point… you may not like what I'm going to say about this, but if you're of the mindset that prophetic utterances and words are uncontrollable words streaming from God through you without any allowed human intervention, then I urge you to do more study on how the Holy Spirit resides in you. You are His temple, and He wants you involved in His actions and ministry. It's God's design in His relationship. In John 3:6, Jesus said:

> "That which is born of the flesh is flesh, and that which is born of the Spirit is spirit."

What this means is His Spirit joining together with our spirit. Both are involved when we are born again.

God does not take full possession of your spirit and mind. It goes against His nature, His plan, and His very purpose, which is to have a relationship. You were made in His image. God's attributes in His creation include His free will established in us. You have been given free will in His image, and He will not violate that.

On the flip side, our adversary, the devil, will violate an unbeliever any chance he gets and, when given the opportunity, may even possess them to some degree. The Bible records cases of evil spirits taking control of individuals. Sometimes demon-possessed people were struck blind or mute or even injured themselves. Consider Matthew 12:22 and Mark 5:2–5. He will also do everything he can to disrupt and disturb a believer's life and spiritual gifts. But he has absolutely no authority over the believer, and his influence has to leave when the believer takes authority over it.

One reason Paul included the discerning of spirits in his list of prophetic gifts in 1 Corinthians 12:10 is for believers to recognize and deal with these influences so their spiritual gifts can flow without obstruction and attack:

> *To another the working of miracles, to another prophecy, to another the ability to distinguish between spirits, to another various kinds of tongues, to another the interpretation of tongues.*

Therefore, the ability to distinguish spirits, as well as having a sensitive heart, a perceptive mind, an observant eye, and a discerning spirit, are all qualities important to the growth of the prophetic gift.

Prophetic Caution

I'm going to interact with you as a reader wanting to know how to move forward with a word from the Lord in the scenario of sharing with leadership. Ready or not here we go ... You might say, "I have this word! I need to give it! It's from God, so it must be important! I'm driven to express this! How do I proceed?"

The above dialogue may sound funny, but engage your mind and your thinking. Engage your reasoning. It's okay. God chose to use you for this word for a reason. He wants to communicate something, He wants to trust you, and He wants to test you. Did I just say He wants to TEST YOU? Yes. Why does He test you? Doesn't He know you'll be obedient?

Name one apostle who got to the point where God stopped testing him. Paul states, "But just as we have been approved by God to be entrusted with the gospel, so we speak, not to please man, but to please God who tests our hearts" (1 Thessalonians 2:4).

Paul also says, "Do not be conformed to this world, but be transformed by the renewal of your mind, that by testing you may discern what is the will of God, what is good and acceptable and perfect" (Romans 12:2). Therefore, testing is a necessary part of the prophetic lifestyle.

You probably know a dozen more verses that will walk right alongside the few mentioned above. However, we tend to forget that God needs to test us with our gifts so we can grow greater with them for His purposes.

My wife is a phenomenal cook, really! But folks, when she started out at the beginning of our marriage, it was hamburger helper and boxed foods. After years in the kitchen, reading, learning, experimenting, failing, reinventing—including plenty of humiliating outcomes—she now presents incredible dinners and dishes that bring healing, love, and joy around our table and beyond. She was given a gift. Through testing, she has profoundly grown to bring glory to God with her talent. That's another whole lesson there, but we'll stick to the subject.

Approaching church leadership, meaning any who have been given the authority to lead, guide, and shape a body of believers from one to a million with a prophetic word from the Lord, takes caution, care, and great respect. Let me share some very practical tools I have found useful in these situations.

To begin with, it would be my suggestion to write it out. Sometimes things take on a different perspective once they are on paper. Does that work for everybody? Probably not. Don't worry—if you heard God, the words will be His. When the words enter your mind, you may have a fear that if you don't speak them when they come, they will disappear. If they are from God, trust that He will keep them there.

Remember, just as He has chosen to use you with your particular language, He has the ability to communicate what He wants on paper just as easily. The Holy Spirit is working with you and through you together. You have to engage your mind to speak in your first language, mine being English. You can also engage your mind to write. We wouldn't have any idea what the prophets said in the Old Testament if they hadn't written down their messages or had a scribe record them.

Another suggestion is to bring the word before others who have a prophetic gift as a trial run of sorts, just as we discussed earlier. Let them consider it. If it's God, and the words are trustworthy, they will approve. But also, be open to their suggestions of how it's to be presented.

If you've done these things, and your heart is right, have a private meeting with your leadership but consider having a colleague with the same gift who agrees with you at the meeting. Sometimes a trustworthy relationship between leadership and the person with a prophetic gift will allow for a direct presentation. But be careful that you are humble and open to being wrong with the word, the timing, or even the tone.

If you do this and your word is rejected, what will you do? If your heart is right, you will do nothing. Let it go. YOU'RE JUST THE MESSENGER. Of course it's sad. It's frustrating, stinky, and can even be alarming. It's God's problem. And the last thing you want is for YOU to be God's problem.

CHAPTER 9

Hearing and Speaking

Communication

It was the late 1980s when I was becoming more active with gifts of knowledge and prophetic words for people. Charismatic circles used the phrase "the word of the Lord" to describe spiritual words from God coming to people's thoughts and minds. It wasn't uncommon to hear a prophetic utterance starting with "thus saith the Lord." It seemed at the time that they used this terminology to distinguish between charismatic churches and non-charismatic, traditional ones. It was used to describe hearing God's voice directly.

During those days, I never gave much thought to it and just figured that was how prophetic people made their declarations publicly. Later in life, I decided to study more about how we use that terminology. I think our words are very important when relaying a message from our God to His people. I discovered that, technically, three Greek words in the New Testament have been translated to English as "word." It is usually not difficult to identify the usage; however, to be thorough, let's take a quick look at two of the three words.

One use of "word" is the Greek word *logos*, which refers to the actual writings of biblical Scripture. Examples where logos refers to Scripture itself are found in Luke 8:11 and Hebrews 4:12. Another use of logos, though, refers to the actual person of Christ Himself, the "Word" used in John 1:1.

"Word" can also be a translation of the Greek word *rhema*, referring to spoken words or a saying. This is the meaning of "word" used in Luke 5:5 when Simon Peter answered Jesus, "Master, we toiled all night and took nothing! But at your word [rhema] I will let down the nets."

As I had mentioned, we can usually understand the usage because it is determined by the historical and biblical narrative.

What does this have to do with the prophetic? Because the prophetic is focused on the communicated rhema from God, we need to be clear about what it is. A great number of Christians do not believe God speaks this way, meaning by way of the Holy Spirit. They will argue God only speaks by His written Word. Some will go "halfway" and say He also speaks through circumstances, but they stop there.

Can God speak in a voice or a perceived voice, as in a conversation? The Bible says He does. And it is clear He does it through the Holy Spirit. Evidence of this is read in Acts 20:22–23: "And now, behold, I am going to Jerusalem, constrained by the Spirit, not knowing what will happen to me there, except that the Holy Spirit testifies [speaks] to me in every city."

Luke also writes about the prophet Agabus:

> *And coming to us, he took Paul's belt and bound his own feet and hands and said, "Thus says the Holy Spirit ..."* (Acts 21:11)

Peter also says:

> *"And I heard a voice saying to me, 'Rise, Peter; kill and eat.'"* (Acts 11:7)

Lastly, Hebrews 3:7 reads:

Therefore, as the Holy Spirit says, "Today, if you hear His voice …"

Therefore, we can see God does and can speak to us directly via the Holy Spirit in this way.

The Lord certainly speaks to us in many ways, but His voice is definitely one of them. As prophetic people, we must always see ourselves as communicators. As communicators, let us make sure we are clear to others about the way God is communicating to us. I believe the Lord loves accuracy. If we have a vision, a dream, an insight, a revelation, a circumstance, or any other way the Lord is communicating, then maybe just say what it is rather than saying "thus saith the Lord."

> *The Lord certainly speaks to us in many ways, but His voice is definitely one of them.*

I will wrap this up by saying God can use your entire being to communicate. Walking in the prophetic is about using all our senses to be in tune with what God wants to communicate to His Church. He may use your physical feeling to tell you about someone else's physical condition, He may use your eyes to see something that triggers what He wants you to pray for, He may use your hearing to do the same, or He may use your imagination to trigger a dream, a vision, or a thought. If you are in tune with His Spirit prophetically, then pay attention to all your senses and keep them before Him for His purposes. He made every little part of you. Surrender access to all of them for His glory and His communication.

CHAPTER 10

Prayer and the Prophet

How Prayer Changed Me

If you don't pray, you're not prophetic. Period.

What's this all about? We all pray if we are Christians, right? We pray in church, we pray at home, we pray on the road, some of us pray everywhere we go. This section is about how prayer matters and affects prophetic people and the messages they forward to others. Remember, prophetic people might be preachers, teachers, counselors, or prayer warriors, as well as people who are spiritually gifted with giving specific prophetic words from God by the Holy Spirit. Here are some of my own experiences to illustrate what can happen when we pray with greater understanding of whom it is we are praying to. This is the heart of the entire book. If you haven't been challenged by what I've written so far, these stories should make a difference in your prophetic calling.

My prophetic gifts changed when I understood and experienced more depth regarding prayer. Simply put, my visions and words got bigger. That may sound strange, but let me explain. At first, I began to notice the influence of what I spoke and what I did when using my prophetic gifting in public settings. The prophetic words and events were becoming more apparent and obvious to others. When I prayed for people, real things, bigger things happened in line with my visions and prayers: healing, enlightened understanding, people finding encouragement and direction, and repentance to accept Jesus.

> *I think the primary purposes of prophecy are to help people return to God, reunite with their Creator and build on that relationship.*

I think the primary purposes of prophecy are to help people return to God, reunite with their Creator and build on that relationship, find a future and a hope, turn from error, and embrace Christ and His kingdom. All kinds of benefits come with those things like greater wisdom, freedom from addictions, finding purpose and hope, and much more.

What do I mean when I say my visions started becoming bigger? They expanded from being one-on-one experiences encouraging individual people or church leaders to becoming regional. The prophetic visions and messages I started receiving were taking on new ground, and a new emphasis was beginning to form. The emphasis was becoming more and more about how to pray for a people group, a region, a nation, and more—prayer that would cause actual change on a large scale.

The visions began to show more about what was coming and what had to change. As an example, the Lord called me to meet with Him in the desert one day, away from all distractions. During that time of intimate worship and prayer, He revealed to me a certain principality over the region. The Lord spoke to me to speak and prophesy against that principality. The words were God's words, declaring Himself as the Great I Am over that place. This principality was about to be brought down.

My vision became so realistic, I wasn't sure if what I saw was in the natural or the Spirit. That principality crashed to the earth in total destruction. Interestingly enough, it also seemed clear to me that this action was not happening in that moment. This was something yet to come. However, the Lord wanted me to speak it out directly to the unseen realm, the spirit realm. Since then, I've had other words about different countries concerning a coming famine or a developing war before those events happened. I've also had positive words for countries regarding agricultural developments or African countries taking a strong role of spiritual leadership and leadership powers shifting.

Along with these kind of messages, I've also had some with more cryptic images I didn't necessarily understand at the time without the help of others. I had to trust the Spirit in me in a greater way because when I'd get a revelation about foreign and national things, things I had no concept of, I had to make a decision whether to believe it or not. I also had to trust that the spiritual visions that were manifesting had biblical foundations.

You may imagine how sometimes a cryptic or symbolic vision, like seeing a white horse rear back three times and then charge forth across a nation, can be a challenge. My discernment has to be turned up very high to be sure I am not being influenced by powers and principalities rebellious to God and ruling the nations.

Receiving these symbolic visions was like a whole new education and training. My gift that had become somewhat comfortable was now becoming more difficult and intense. It became a burden I felt in a deeper way. Frankly, I was timid and fearful at first. However, not to sound proud or arrogant,

I know His voice, and I know His way with me and my gift. I still hold firmly to Proverbs 15:22 that says the counsel of many is wise.

Not a Typical Prayer

A new focus on prayer emphasizes aspects such as time, intensity, place, worship, acknowledgment, surrender, and humility. Consider, too, intangible words, the ones you cannot formulate with your primary language, also connected with prayer. These are the words that come out as emotions, groans, tears, and, yes, tongues which surpass our human understanding.

I have a close friend, Jay, who is also one of my accountability partners. He meets with me quite often and challenges me, listens to me, and always holds my feet to the fire, meaning he holds everything I talk about up to the Bible as a standard. Jay is a very strong Bible teacher. He has a firm grasp of how to study the historical, hermeneutics, and exegesis of Scripture. I think he carries his references around with him wherever he goes.

One thing I love about Jay is I can describe some ridiculous or strange experience I might have in prayer or a dream, and he will dig right into it and begin relating to it with his profound thoughts and his own experiences. Then he will surround it with the written Word. So often we connect on that level. The reason is we both want the same thing. We want to be as close to God as we can. We want to be used by God to our fullest, and we want to know Him to whatever capacity our hearts and minds will allow. One other thing we have in common is our prayer lives.

We've discovered what it means to continually reach out to the Holy Spirit and ask for a greater two-way depth and a greater two-way impact. What do I mean? I'm sure you realize prayer is a two-way communication. We all want what we say to God to have greater depth and impact, but do we ever ask God to have greater depth and impact back to us? If so, how far will we let Him go?

Believe me, I know people who can get really emotional in prayer. Emotion is not what I'm talking about. All Christians should give everything to their prayer times, and prophetic people should give even more.

The prophet King David tried really hard to express the depth of his prayers in his psalms: deep, heart-wrenching prayers as well as ecstatic and joyful ones. Can we see his prayerful heart in his psalms? Let's see if we can understand his heart and mind when he prays. Look at the first five verses of David's Psalm 108. These verses record what David experiences when he prays to Yahweh:

> *My heart is steadfast, O God! I will sing and make melody with all my being! Awake, O harp and lyre! I will awake the dawn! I will give thanks to you, O LORD, among the peoples; I will sing praises to you among the nations. For your steadfast love is great above the heavens; your faithfulness reaches to the clouds. Be exalted, O God, above the heavens! Let your glory be over all the earth!*

What do you think is in David's heart and mind when he prays those five short verses? David begins his time in prayer with worship. Worship is so important. He shows us how to begin prayer, by blessing God! We should always do this at the start of our prayers. David wakes up and feels the adrenaline of his spirit. It's so strong with the Holy Spirit he must praise and worship in his morning prayer. He is uninhibited because with all his heart and mind he is devoted to blessing God with his love and honor for Him. Complete adoration. He cares not that others are witnessing him.

As David moves through his blessing to God, he then acknowledges the love God has for him. When David says, "For your steadfast love is great above the heavens," he's saying God's love is incomprehensible; it is above the cosmos, the universe, the entirety of all known creation. This is because of its limitless nature—God's love has no boundaries. Yet, He shares that love with our human hearts and minds to the highest capacity that we are able to perceive it, going ever deeper as our relationship with Him deepens and grows.

"Your faithfulness reaches to the clouds" (v. 4). God's faithfulness is infinite. It breaks all human boundaries, not confined by time or space. Its depth never ends, and its height never stops.

He wants us to continually pursue and experience that kind of faith in Him. Boundless faith. Let that sink in—faith without boundaries. (Can we have this kind of faith when we pray? The answer is yes, it's available to us.)

"Be exalted ... above the heavens" (v. 5). David is reminding, even commanding, his own heart and mind to lift up and acknowledge God as the supreme Creator. David can scarcely comprehend God's infinite greatness to the point that he acknowledges God is above the heavens, which is a reflection of His supreme omniscience in the cosmos.

"Let Your glory be over all the earth" (v. 5). David is crying out (singing out) in a heart overtaken and consumed with the Holy Spirit, saying "Lord, show yourself!" He longs for the very appearance of the Great I Am. Essentially, he's asking God to come! (Perhaps, he's even longing for the Messiah.)

That's just the beginning of David's prayer before he moves into his request. David does this regularly when he prays. He begins with worship for God in his prayer. He humbles and empties himself while blessing God. Are we doing that? This is how David finds himself in the presence of God. He understands he must enter into the unseen realm of the divine council, the heavenly hosts, and the throne room of God if he wants to know what God wants and what he can ask of God.

David had an understanding of God that started as a child in the fields tending sheep. He discovered how faith gave him access to the presence of God. God honored and blessed David with that access. This kind of faith is based in a deep, personal relationship with God and builds into the prophetic nature He (God) gives to a person.

I want to give a biblical foundation to what I just said, found in Jeremiah 23:18:

> *For who among them has stood in the council of the LORD [the divine council] to see and to hear his word, or who has paid attention to his word and listened?*

In Job 15:7–9, we read:

> *"Are you the first man who was born? Or were you brought forth before the hills? Have you listened to the council [the divine council] of God? And do you limit wisdom to yourself? What do you know that we do not know? What do you understand that is not clear to us?"*

The pronouns "we" and "us" clarify that these are divine or spiritual beings that make up the council and heavenly hosts of Yahweh.

We want our prayers to be heard and answered in the presence of the Lord. Through Jesus, that's possible. There are probably thousands of sermons and teachings on the Lord's Prayer. But just read that one line, "Your kingdom come, your will be done, on earth as it is in heaven" (Matthew 6:10). He shows us the "here but not yet." We have access, but we aren't complete. We learn in the presence of God in prayer that the heavenly or spiritual dimension can be carried out here on earth. That's the nature of the prophet and the prophetic in prayer.

CHAPTER 11

The New Testament Prophet

Traditional American Reasoning

Making distinctions between a person who gives a prophetic word and a person called to the position or the office of a prophet brings out fears, struggles, frustrations, and even fights. Much of the American traditional church will immediately dismiss anyone being called a prophet in today's modern era. In Africa, meanwhile, hundreds, if not thousands, of church leaders are called prophets and apostles. Are all these leaders really biblical prophets and apostles? I can guess the answer is not likely; however, this distinction shows a cultural difference in the understanding and the role of this office given in Old and New Testament scriptures.

In America primarily, and perhaps other Western nations, a traditional perspective of the Gospel and the Bible as a whole came out of the Age of Reason. The Age of Reason, or the Enlightenment, was an intellectual movement that began in Europe in the seventeenth and eighteenth centuries. The movement involved philosophers and scientists who relied mainly on reason, observation, and experimentation to reach conclusions and who believed that the world and humanity could be rationally studied and explained.

Their perspective made it difficult for them to accept things they could not understand or reason with. This view of Scripture sought to reason away any idea of the activity of the Holy Spirit and the continuation of the spiritual gifts listed in several different places in the Bible.

Here are the basics of how this reasoning is taught: They usually begin with Ephesians 4:11–12:

> *And He Himself gave some to be apostles, some prophets, some evangelists, and some pastors and teachers, for the equipping of the saints for the work of ministry, for the edifying of the body of Christ.* (NKJV)

This cessationist view is focused on the word "gave." Cessationists believe this word is in the past tense, indicating that the gifts of the prophetic and apostles ended with the twelve apostles. They justify the gifts of teaching, preaching, and evangelism because of what 1 Timothy 3 and Titus 1 say about elders and deacons having qualifications for those ministries. Therefore, their conclusion is those offices should continue. They claim the continuation of these ministries is how the Word will spread.

However, nothing is mentioned in those particular verses about prophets or apostles. They assume or speculate Paul is saying that these extraordinary offices were only for that foundation-laying period of the church. They claim Paul is saying prophets and apostles were necessary to bring the church to maturity—to adulthood—but now we only need pastors and teachers who build on that foundation and lead us through Scripture so we will stand in the day of Jesus Christ. They actually will state that because of the accomplishment of redemption and the work of Jesus Christ, we have no need for new or fresh revelation.

Obviously, I'm abbreviating their argument, but that's it in a nutshell. I'm sure you can find others who will bring more scripture verses into the defense. However, their argument just doesn't stand without making a great deal of assumptions and speculations not in context in the Bible.

In my own personal opinion, I think their view is driven by the fear of things they can't understand and control, including the fear of disturbing institutionalized structures. So they need to explain the prophetic away and decide it no longer exists. Yet it does.

I wonder sometimes what they do when spiritual gifts, like words of knowledge, prophetic words that come to pass, or an apostleship that takes place when a leader exhibits all the gifts in his five-fold ministry, are active. What do they do with these types of current-day examples? I am also somewhat amazed at the limitations they put on themselves and their followers for ministry in proclaiming the Gospel and reaching the world for Christ, the ultimate reasons for distributing those gifts.

New Testament Prophets

What about someone being an actual prophet? I'm describing an official position or office of a prophet, not talking about someone who just gives a prophetic word. I'll focus on that later. The office of a prophet is a calling in a specific spiritual gift recognized as an appointed position from God and understood by church leadership.

Some very important verses from the Bible reveal more about the office of the prophet. Using the same verse the cessationists use, Paul writes this in Ephesians 4:11–12:

> *And He Himself gave [offers, grants, gives] some to be apostles, some prophets, some evangelists, and some*

pastors and teachers, for the equipping of the saints for the work of ministry, for the edifying [building up] of the body of Christ ... (NKJV)

He also writes this in 1 Corinthians 12:28-31:

And God has appointed in the church first apostles, second prophets, third teachers, then miracles, then gifts of healing, helping, administrating, and various kinds of tongues. Are all apostles? Are all prophets? Are all teachers? Do all work miracles? Do all possess gifts of healing? Do all speak with tongues? Do all interpret? But earnestly desire the higher gifts.

Luke gives an account of prophets other than the twelve apostles in Acts 11:27-28:

Now in these days prophets came down from Jerusalem to Antioch. And one of them named Agabus stood up and foretold by the Spirit that there would be a great famine over all the world.

And for the unbeliever, the fulfillment of Agabus's words is recorded in history in the days of Claudius.

Agabus was with a group of prophets traveling together. Being in a group seems to be a very common thread in the New Testament. (For example, Acts 13 records a group of prophets.) In Acts 21, Agabus shows up again with a group of prophets.

In the New Testament church, we should realize God gave the prophet to the ecclesia, the whole body of Christian believers, because the prophet is needed for helping the church reach maturity.

Rick Renner of Renner Ministries discusses the idea in his book *Apostles & Prophets* that today's Christian circles widely misuse the term "prophet." The title is often misunderstood and incorrectly assigned. Many people can be drawn to the prophetic and give prophecy, but that does not mean they are a Christ-given Prophet.[1]

I'm going to jump in and clarify that a church congregation or any group of believers does NOT appoint a prophet. God appoints prophets! Prophets are real. So, where are they? I tend to believe there really aren't very many genuine prophets compared to how many proclaim or profess to hold the office. In my fifty years of Christian service, I've only met two or three real prophets in the circles I've traveled. The New Testament does mention groups of prophets, although we know very little about them.

In Acts 13, Antioch was a hub of prophetic gathering. We're only given a few names out of the group in Acts 13:1:

> Now there were in the church at Antioch prophets and teachers, Barnabas, Simeon who was called Niger, Lucius of Cyrene, Manaen a lifelong friend of Herod the tetrarch, and Saul.

Certain parts in the Greek text indicate the order of the first three were prophets and the last two were teachers. This means Barnabas, Simeon, and Lucius functioned primarily as prophets, while Manaen and Saul were teachers.

But 2 Timothy 1:11 records Paul's ministry expanding. Paul clarifies he was appointed as a "preacher and apostle and teacher." In this context. the same Greek term for "preacher" doubles for "prophet," which means Paul also was given to the prophetic ministry, as a five-fold ministry needed for apostleship. At the very least, we know he functioned with a prophetic gift.

Agabus Reveals the Future

In Acts 11:27, Agabus shows up with his group, who are revealing divine mysteries and foretelling events to come. Acts 11:28 (KJV) tells us that Agabus "signified," which means he gave an alert or a signal, in this case of a dramatic foretelling of a drought. Agabus was empowered by the Spirit.

What actually took place? Agabus was ready. He was open and sensitive to the move or message the Holy Spirit needed to speak. He had his antenna up. Agabus gave his prophecy, and the group with him listened and confirmed it. The people listening then took up a collection and prepared themselves for what was to come. They trusted and believed Agabus. And the prophecy took place.

In Acts 21, we meet Philip and his daughters. Philip is an evangelist living in Caesarea. Philip has four daughters, to whom Christ had each given a special prophetic gift and the office of prophetess. We read this story in Acts 21:8–10:

> *On the next day we departed and came to Caesarea, and we entered the house of Philip the evangelist, who was one of the seven, and stayed with him. He had four unmarried daughters, who prophesied. While we were staying for many days, a prophet named Agabus came down from Judea.*

In this verse, "one of the seven" likely means he was one of the original disciples to take the Gospel to the Gentiles, including the Ethiopian church. The text says these women prophesied. I'm told the way it is written emphasizes "amazingly" or "emphatically." The idea is these four daughters were recognized as well-known prophetic women, who may have been operating in the office as prophetesses.

Extra-historical biblical books from Josephus and others give testimony to New Testament prophets meeting up with each other, working together, and traveling to join each other. Considering that prophetic people were often in groups may lend more credence as to why Paul taught on the manner and order of prophetic conduct in the church.

In Acts 21:10–11, Agabus shows up at the house of Philip and gives a word from the Holy Spirit about what will happen to Paul:

> *And coming to us, he took Paul's belt and bound his own feet and hands and said, "Thus says the Holy Spirit, 'This is how the Jews at Jerusalem will bind the man who owns this belt and deliver him into the hands of the Gentiles.'"*

Agabus didn't limit his communication to words alone. He acted out what the Holy Spirit was showing him, similar to Old Testament prophets like Ezekiel. Notice that the word didn't come to the others who were there, such as the women prophets.

> *Agabus didn't limit his communication to words alone.*

When the Holy Spirit speaks through different people, the others are to listen, carefully assess the given word, and stay quiet. This process allows others to hear and respond to the message with approval or not.

The lesson in that is not to build on other people's prophecies. Paul instructed this lesson in 1 Corinthians 14:32:

> *The spirits of the prophets are subject to the prophets.*

I also think this shows the maturity of Agabus's ministry. Others saw Agabus as a senior prophet among prophets.

We can understand from these kind of scenes that we need a prophetic ministry group in our churches so we can see and walk in the whole counsel of God.

We can also read about more New Testament prophets. Acts 15:32 tells us:

> And Judas and Silas, who were themselves prophets, encouraged and strengthened the brothers with many words.

Such a great move of the Spirit was happening in Antioch that the Jerusalem church felt it important to send more prophets for the sake of guidance, encouragement, and building up the body of believers. Paul and Barnabas were there teaching and preaching. However, the church needed more to keep up the strength of what was happening, give supernatural revelation, and foretell things to come, like the famine Agabus foretold in Acts 11:28.

We can read more about prophetic actions in the early church that include New Testament ordinations. They were not like our American church ordinations today. When it was time for Timothy to be ordained, the elders laid hands on him and prayed and prophesied over him. Read 1 Timothy 1:18–19:

> This charge I entrust to you, Timothy, my child, in accordance with the prophecies previously made about you, that by them you may wage the good warfare, holding faith and a good conscience.

Read also in 1 Timothy 4:14:

> Do not neglect the gift you have, which was given you by prophecy when the council of elders laid their hands on you.

This verse may be showing that among the council of elders were unnamed prophets. Prophets were considered a necessary part of the church leadership.

Building Trust

A challenge for the church today is learning how to recognize those who are actually called to the office of a prophet. Remember, the church does not appoint them, but they can recognize them and then honor their gift just like they do for the teacher, the preacher, the evangelist, and the other appointed five-fold ministries. Trust is a big issue when it comes to prophetic gifting—trust from church leaders and church attenders. I think this trust issue has a great deal to do with the lack of education regarding spiritual gifts. To add to that, though, the church has not allowed much display to prove the authenticity of prophetic gifts.

CHAPTER 12

Non-Prophet Prophecies

God can use anyone to prophesy. Some people like to point to Numbers 22:21–39 and say if God can use a donkey to speak to Balaam, then God can use anybody. That story may be humorous, but remember, donkeys are not made in God's image, and we are. On a side note, people may act like donkeys, but that's why Christ came ... to set them free from being ... well, you know.

Donkeys aside, the prophetic really isn't a joking matter. The prophetic involves the words and actions of our Creator. Our God deserves the highest reverence.

Let's make this personal: All Christians should have a prayerful and interactive relationship with God because of the sacrifice of Jesus Christ that brought them into salvation and back into relationship with God the Father. Because of His unconditional love, Jesus said that we can be filled with His Spirit. If you are not sure if you are, then ask someone to pray with you for that to happen.

The new believers in Samaria had just given their lives to follow Jesus but weren't experiencing the power of the Holy Spirit. We read about the Samarian believers receiving the Holy Spirit in Acts 8:14–17:

Now when the apostles at Jerusalem heard that Samaria had received the word of God, they sent to them Peter and John, who came down and prayed for them that they might receive the Holy Spirit, for he had not yet fallen on any of them, but they had only been baptized in the name of the Lord Jesus. Then they laid their hands on them and they received the Holy Spirit.

This passage clearly shows that they believed and were baptized in water only. They were not filled or baptized with the Holy Spirit until Peter and John prayed for them. They needed the baptism of the Holy Spirit so the power of the Lord could be active in them. It is by His power that people can be truly transformed. How can people grow in the spiritual gifts if the Gift Giver is not activated in them? Who gives the gifts of the Spirit?

> *Gifts come from the Holy Spirit, and He activates or "manifests" them as He sees fit.*

Consider that the gifts come from the Holy Spirit, and He activates or "manifests" them as He sees fit. When He finds an open vessel (someone willing to hear and walk in obedience), He might just choose that person to speak for God. And if that person is someone who learns or knows how to manage that gift in such a way that God is honored and glorified, then that gift might become a recurring gift in that person's life. That is called prophecy.

Did I just make an assumption or a speculation? Not really. In 1 Peter, Peter talks to the group of Christians scattered through Asia Minor with encouragement and instruction concerning their availability of speaking prophetically. First Peter 4:10–11 says:

> *As each has received a gift, use it to serve one another, as good stewards of God's varied grace: whoever speaks,*

as one who speaks oracles of God; whoever serves, as one who serves by the strength that God supplies—in order that in everything God may be glorified through Jesus Christ.

Paul Encourages Prophecy

All of 1 Corinthians 14 is filled with encouragement about everyone speaking prophetically. Rather than me writing out the whole chapter, please read it. Again, Paul is not addressing the prophet specifically. Paul is asking everyone to be open to the prophetic gift, whether it happens as a one-time event or repeatedly. In 1 Corinthians 14:3 (NKJV), he writes:

But he who prophesies speaks edification and exhortation and comfort to men.

Paul stresses the incredible importance of prophecy for the building up and encouragement of the church body.

Is Paul writing about prophets foretelling future events? No, he isn't. He's writing about prophecy as an understanding and a revealing of mysteries. In 1 Corinthians 14:5 (NKJV), he writes:

I wish you all spoke with tongues, but even more that you prophesied.

Paul is speaking to "all."

What kind of words might these prophecies be? They might be revelation on a personal level such as setting someone free from a stronghold or a harassing spirit. It could also be prophetic at a corporate level, bringing joy, peace, encouragement, and hope. In the midst of trials and challenges, receiving such an encouraging word can be the difference between staying in relationship or walking away from Jesus.

Often when difficulties come to a person or to a corporate body of believers, our adversary jumps in full force and tries to destroy every inch of growth and relationship. He brings disappointment, discouragement, and division. Too many times I've seen this. Then a word comes from the Lord though an individual, and the light of God breaks through the dark cloud of the event. Through that prophetic word, God reveals His purpose, His plan, or just plain wisdom that's beyond our typical understanding. As a result, the freedom of the Spirit inspires believers to worship, to praise, and to be strengthened in their walk with God. It's a hallelujah moment!

Prior to the significant teaching Paul reveals in 1 Corinthians 14, he gives us an absolute which all the gifts must be established in. He explains to us in 1 Corinthians 13 the key purpose of any gift by the Holy Spirit is LOVE! All our gifts from God are useless without love. Love is not a magical, euphoric feeling that comes over you and somehow accompanies your gift. Sorry, but love is something we have to learn, practice, struggle for, surrender to, and embrace in our most difficult times and search out in our relationship with God and each other.

He is the author of agape love, the love that surpasses our own abilities but accompanies us by His Spirit when we are exhausted, empty, and sometimes frustrated to anger. Agape love is the love we need when we use our spiritual gifts. It is unconditional. And when we are really unhappy with someone, and the Lord wants to speak into that situation or circumstance, we have to be able to lean on that love. The fact is the entire Bible has an overall message, which is God's love to all of us.

Prophecy Preserved This Church

Here is a real example of people being inspired through the spiritual gift of prophecy regarding a serious problem that happened in a church where I was on staff.

It came to light that our married pastor was having an affair with our worship leader's wife. This situation was tragic, to say the least, but certainly not uncommon. The difficulty was in the surrounding circumstances. He was a very loved pastor. He preached effective messages and had personal, strong relationships in the congregation of about 500 people. He had built that church up from a very small beginning and had been the lead pastor for about ten years.

I was on the board of elders at the time, and a division ensued among the elders. Half the board wanted him to repent and keep preaching, and the other half wanted him to resign. This issue grew even worse and more intense when that division was announced to the church body. (I was not part of that decision.) As you can imagine, now the entire church was divided.

What a mess. How would God resolve this and keep the body together and encouraged after such an event?

Time for the prophetic people, the counselors, the teachers—and the pastor who sinned—to all come together and seek God for His resolution. It was a challenging situation. To be clear, the pastor was repentant and had stopped the affair, but we needed help. We all spent time in prayer, and suddenly, something dynamic and prophetic came forth from that meeting. Someone spoke a word of revelation that had to do with being focused on the wrong issues. Someone else spoke out about something that seemed completely unrelated. Someone else spoke another word that was a revelation regarding the worship leader and his wife.

It turned out the "unrelated" word hit the nail on the head and convicted the pastor to reveal a continual, hidden sin that was behind the affair.

These revelations were things that no one had known or considered. A couple more words of wisdom came forth on how to proceed that no one had thought of or considered. In summary, everything that was revealed in that meeting lined up perfectly with Scripture, and when the meeting ended, there was agreement and peace. There was unity, and there was a plan.

I'm avoiding details for safeguarding, but I hope you're following my purpose in my example to see the need for prophecy in the church. Surprisingly, part of the plan God wanted to go forward with involved the pastor himself speaking to the church, revealing his sin, and publicly repenting of his sin, and then resigning. But the resignation was for a time to heal and be restored back into alignment with Christ. This was for discovering things for him personally and for his family's life.

The worship leader and his wife chose to leave the church and the region as soon as the affair was discovered. Sadly, they fell apart. That was the aftermath of such a tragic situation and not part of the plan prophesied. They ended in divorce. They didn't want counsel or help to find a way through, and their situation took the direction as expected.

Restoration

After the pastor repented publicly, what happened in the church body was amazing. Repentance moved through the body and, for some, private confession of their own sexual sin. There was also repentance of accusation and maligned judgment between believers. There were tears, there was prayer, and there was worship. There was an amazing unity of love, acceptance, and a heartfelt need to hold each other close. God also brought marriages closer together and restored them, as couples saw the wake-up call and renewed their focus of how important it is to have Jesus Christ in the center of their marriage relationship. A cleansing went through that church during that time, now twenty-five years ago.

The pastor's marriage was even restored, and, after a few years, the pastor was able to use his gifts in a new setting. Having met with him, I was truly blessed that he was strong in the Lord once again. The main church is going strong today and continuing in the purpose God had from the beginning.

The point here is that whether it is a recognized prophet or a person simply open to the word and revelation of the Holy Spirit, these gifts are very important to have in the church body. They simply need to be encouraged, watched, guided, embraced, and taught with biblical wisdom.

CHAPTER 13

Continuing with My Prophetic Gift

To conclude my thoughts on the prophetic, let's pick up my personal journey from chapter nine and bring it to the present. God has brought my prophetic gift into a new expansion. Let's ask a few questions of this expansion: Why am I now getting words to prophesy to entire regions or more? And whom am I prophesying to?

One morning, around 4:30 a.m., I was sitting in the dark on my couch, praying as I often do, when I received a prompting from the Holy Spirit. The prompt came in the form of a vision. In the vision, I was walking in the desert. I live in Arizona, so that was no big stretch of the imagination.

In the vision, I was alone, crying out to God because He was filling me with a message. While sitting on that couch, still enraptured by the vision, I heard His voice asking me to meet with Him in the literal desert. So I promptly headed out in my four-by-four, aimlessly asking Him to point the way. All I did was follow my basic instincts and ideas for a place to go off-road and look for somewhere to park. I had no dramatic spiritual revelation as to where He wanted me. Instead, it was just me picking a spot away from any distractions. In reflection, I believe that was God's intent for this desert wandering, to get me away from all the distractions and interruptions.

I left the vehicle and started to do what I call a walkabout. I just began walking about the desert, praying, worshiping, and basically doing what David did, giving all of himself to bless the Lord. Soon, I found a rock, and I sat in silence.

Alas, I heard His voice, like I so often do, with His usual introduction. He always says, "I love you." And, of course, I say it back, usually with tears in my eyes. (Like in my visitation vision in chapter five.) When you hear the voice of God tell you He loves you, you practically shake inside because that revelation is infinitely deep.

Once I hear His greeting, He then begins to give me visions accompanied with words. But now, these visions are different and expanded. Now, they have national and global pictures, not the usual more local and personal visions I'm used to. These visions have the condition of nations, and some involve the state of my own country.

Within the vision, He reveals what is happening and how and His ultimate plan for what needs to take place. He reveals His purposes, His desired outcomes, and His leadings on where things will go. Some of His revelation is about the physical world but has a central focus on the spiritual. He reveals battle scenes over certain regions and whom those battles are with. He presents me with details I had no previous knowledge of. And He tells me He wants me to participate in what is going on.

This was definitely new territory for me. I learned that because He asked me to participate, He was asking me to prophesy against certain powers and principalities. He would tell me what to say. He gave me words to declare to the spirit-realm powers that their time and their activity was coming to an end and that God was bringing disruption and destruction to their powers and activities. As we know from the Word, eventually they will fall.

For example, in my vision, I even saw one of them crashing to the earth in the future. Since I'm in the habit of writing everything down, I submitted my experience to several others that hold me accountable in my walk and my gift. I have five primary people who walk beside me in these things; two are strong prophetic believers and teachers (one is a messianic Jewish brother), another is a strong teacher and pastor, the fourth is a strong prayer warrior, and the final one is a scrutinizer who will tear my word apart if he can. All are mature and proficient in the study of the Bible.

My experience in the desert has happened a number of times where God has called me back there for walkabouts. Each time God has a different message, but they are always on a national and world scale. A few have been spiritually cryptic, and I believe they will show their meaning when the time is right. But I hold all of them up to the Word for alignment, meaning biblical validity, understanding, and some kind of confirmation in the heart and spirit that comes with God's presence and revelation through the Bible.

> *Hold all of them up to the Word for alignment, meaning biblical validity, understanding, and some kind of confirmation*

So, what should someone do when they receive words like these? I don't believe they are always for sharing publicly, especially on a large public platform. They come less as a warning and more as direction and comfort. They are words that reveal God's love, His power, His omniscience, His plans, His encouragement, His wisdom, and His security with us in Him. They are words that proclaim righteousness and sometimes give spiritual preparedness for events or spiritual battles we will encounter. They also give insight and confirmation to the listener that God has you in His arms and trusts you with the things He wants to say.

Who, then, gets to read these words? In my case, the five people I am accountable to. Then, if they feel others should hear these things, I give that responsibility to each of them. If I am confident the Holy Spirit wants me to share the message with others who can handle these things, then they might also see them. His word will go forth to those whom He desires to hear it and who will seek Him for understanding.

Recapping Prophetic Purposes and Qualifications

I must clarify that prophecy by believers, no matter what, does NOT form the basis of Scripture. It is not inspired in the sense that it can be added to the Bible. That work is finished and established. If anyone says differently, run away.

Prophecy in the New Testament is never the basis for the development of doctrine. Doctrine proceeds from the knowledge of Christ and from deep examination of Scripture—in a sensible and reasoned fashion.

Next, prophecy and prophets in the world are going to increase whether you're ready for it or not. It's going to happen. I don't have to be a prophet to proclaim that. It's scriptural. However, in my spirit, I sense this pouring out (although it began with Jesus) will greatly increase and will be happening exponentially very soon, so we must be ready. Acts 2:17–18 is very clear about it:

> "And in the last days it shall be, God declares, that I will pour out my Spirit on all flesh, and your sons and your daughters shall prophesy, and your young men shall see visions, and your old men shall dream dreams; even on my male servants and female servants in those days I will pour out my Spirit, and they shall prophesy."

Recapping, here are four quick purposes of prophecy:

1. For edification, exhortation, and comfort.
2. To bring conviction and repentance to unbelievers.
3. To impart spiritual gifts and the sending out of missionaries.
4. To warn about upcoming events that might be immediate so Christians can take the correct course of action, like Agabus did concerning the drought in Acts 11:28.

When all is said and done, we have to take into account some important signs of so-called prophets that are red flags. Seeing these red flags would indicate a "prophet" to avoid or be concerned about.

1. A person calling himself or herself a prophet but who is looking for a profit.
2. A prophet who does not associate with a Christ-centered church authority.
3. A prophet who only speaks on "spiritual experiences" and "revelations," not the Bible.
4. A prophet who "grandstands," making proclamations for attention.
5. Any prophet who is obviously living in sin.

Consider the qualifications of the true prophet discussed in this book.

The Journey Continues

My journey is just that, a journey. It is never-ending until I enter the fullness of His presence in heaven. I will always be learning, studying, experiencing, growing, and hopefully maturing as a believer in the gift God shares with me. We are all sons and daughters of the Most High. Praise and worship be to our Father, the King of Kings, the Lord of Lords, the Almighty I AM.

I submit this final verse to encourage you to do a deep dive and see what it reveals to you. Hopefully, it will make a difference in how you understand the role of the prophetic in today's church.

Ephesians 2:18–22:

> For through Him we both have access in one Spirit to the Father. So then you are no longer strangers and aliens, but you are fellow citizens with the saints and members of the household of God, built on the foundation of the apostles and prophets, Christ Jesus himself being the cornerstone, in whom the whole structure, being joined together, grows into a holy temple in the Lord. In Him, you also are being built together into a dwelling place for God by the Spirit.

FINAL THOUGHTS

Where Do We Go from Here?

Churches or members of churches that operate with the five-fold ministry gifts of the Holy Spirit are lucky to have the kind of ministry and freedom to excitingly watch the Gospel advance with their mission. These ministry gifts can certainly be challenging from a leadership point of view and can be difficult to oversee. However, the rewards can be absolutely amazing for the church body.

Many churches struggle with incorporating all the gifts of the Spirit, and understandably so. People are unpredictable, bruised, beat up, socially confused; some are mentally unstable or have difficult personalities. But we are not called to a spirit of fear (2 Timothy 1:7).

To hold back the spiritual gifts is like admitting you are afraid of what people might do with them. We need to teach them, train them, and encourage them if we want to see the fullness of the ministry take place in our churches. There will be rocky times, rough roads, and difficult decisions in the process. But trusting in the Lord and relying on His wisdom will smooth them out.

A time is coming when it won't matter what we fear or what we think about the gifts of the Spirit because God is going to pour out His Spirit upon all flesh (Joel 2:28). Whether we are ready or not, the gifts will happen. Things will happen in your church you don't expect. People will speak out, will be overcome, will have dreams and visions.

They will see things they never saw before and experience things they didn't know were possible. What will you do? How will you respond?

Revivals will arise, and people seeking and searching for answers will flock to them. They will witness the gifts of the Spirit. They will ask church leaders to help them, guide them, and answer what is happening. What will those leaders say, and how will they guide them?

A well-trained staff will know what to do and how to answer the call. People who are mature with a spiritual gift will have the direction and understanding of how to lead and guide.

An exciting journey is ahead of us. God loves us with a great and mighty love. God wants to restore us back to Him. He wants to share His attributes with us. He is a family man and wants to reunite His heavenly family with His earthly one in the finale. That has been His intended desire from the beginning of creation.

Let's be ready and prepared with our spiritual gifts as these last days unfold.

Lastly, look through your church body and consider whom God has brought into your midst. Do you have leaders attending that aren't being acknowledged? Do you have people with the gifts of the Spirit who aren't being acknowledged? Your first step might just be to meet one-on-one with those people and learn who they are and what they understand about the gifts they have. As Paul encouraged Timothy, encourage those with spiritual gifts to train, learn, and grow with guidance into mature believers, fanning the flame and actively building up the body of Christ.

Endnotes

Chapter 1

1. *Collins Dictionary.com*, s.v. "journey," accessed September 23, 2023, https://www.collinsdictionary.com/dictionary/english/journey.

Chapter 3

1. "Měrsay," Hebrew word defined in the Logos Bible Study Platform (Logos 10, 2022), Lexicon section.
2. Michael S. Heiser, "Prophets Weren't Psychics, They Were Covenant Enforcers," YouTube, November 15, 2021, https://www.youtube.com/watch?v=-zLo0t63TjAU, 1:54 minute mark.
3. Gordon D. Fee and Douglas Stuart, *How to Read the Bible for All Its Worth*, Fourth Edition, (Grand Rapids, MI: Zondervan, 2014), chapters 9–10.
4. John Barry, Logos Bible Study Platform (Logos 10, 2022), found in the *Faithlife Study Bible* commentary section for Deuteronomy 18:22 under the heading "A New Prophet Like Moses."

Chapter 4

1. John Barry, Logos Bible Study Platform (Logos 10, 2022), found in the *Faithlife Study Bible* commentary section under the heading "Micaiah Prophesies Against Ahab."
2. Michael Willemse, "Who Were the Old Testament Prophets?", *Christian Study Library*, https://www.christianstudylibrary.org/article/who-were-old-testament-prophets, 2014.

3. Michael S. Heiser, Logos Bible Study Platform (Logos 10, 2022), found in the *Faithlife Study Bible* commentary section under the heading "Introduction to Joel."
4. John Barry, Logos Bible Study Platform (Logos 10, 2022), found in the *Faithlife Study Bible* commentary section under the heading "Jesus Fulfills the Law."

Chapter 7

1. Michael S. Heiser, *Naked Bible Podcast* (Ezekiel series), https://nakedbiblepodcast.com.
2. Alexander Souter, *A Pocket Lexicon to the Greek New Testament* (Oxford: Clarendon Press, 1922), p. 147.

Chapter 11

1. Rick Renner, *Apostles & Prophets* (Shippensburg, PA: Harrison House, 2022), Chapter 7, "What Is a Prophet?"

Additional Resources for Further Study

Bolinger, Hope. March 20, 2020. "What Is the Rhema Word?" Christianity.com. https://christianity.com/wiki/bible/what-is-the-rhema-word.html.

Bucher, Meg. January 27, 2022. "What Does the Bible Say about the Gift of Prophecy?" Crosswalk.com. https://www.crosswalk.com/faith/bible-study/what-does-the-bible-say-about-the-gift-of-prophecy.html.

Cantor, Ron. April 11, 2020. "12 Principles on New Testament Prophets." roncantor.com/post/12-principles-on-new-testament-prophets.

Floyd, Michael H. and Robert D. Haak, eds. 2006. *Prophets, Prophecy, and Prophetic Texts in Second Temple Judaism.* London: Bloomsbury T&T Clark.

Horton, Michael. March 18, 2022. "FAQ: Are There Apostles and Prophets today?" Core Christianity. https://corechristianity.com/resources/articles/faq-are-there-prophets-and-apostles-today.

The International Inductive Study Bible. 1993. Eugene, OR: Harvest House Publishers.

"The Rhema Word—What Is It?" n.d. Compelling Truth. https://www.compellingtruth.org/rhema-word.html, Accessed 15 October 2023.

Storms, Sam. October 8, 2015. "What Does Scripture Teach About the Office of Prophet and Gift of Prophecy?" The Gospel Coalition. thegospelcoalition.org/article/sam-storms-what-does-scripture-teach-about-office-prophet-gift-prophecy.

About the Author

Bill Arnold was born and raised in Wisconsin before his spiritual journey and commitment to the Lord grabbed hold of his life. God took Bill's rough childhood and turned it into an amazing relationship of love, peace, and the pursuit of understanding God and His gifts.

Bill often talks about his missions and the miracles he was blessed to witness and be a part of, as well as the different cultures his adventures took him on. His short-term missions allowed him to travel to ten different countries to share the Gospel, work in positions of service for ministries, and experience everything from language barriers to praying with people in the midst of temples erected for the kingdom of darkness.

During Bill's time with YWAM, he enrolled in the University of Nations and set course for graduating with a ministry degree, only to fall short by one class. Later in life, Bill returned to school for a BA degree in graphic design and graduated with honors. Along the way, he took on a leadership role as a youth pastor for several years. He served on church boards as an elder and learned all the inner workings of church managing, structure, and decision-making.

Bill also worked in home construction and as a grade-school art teacher, a graphic designer for a vendor to Nike, and, later in life, a school bus driver. Bill and his wife, Carin, raised three kids and one foster daughter and live near Phoenix, Arizona. By now, seven grandkids have entered the family and are the apple of Bill's eye.

Bill's ministry continues through his local church, where he ministers one-on-one and in small group meetings, a prophetic group, a men's group, and a prayer ministry. He also serves in his church's community outreach program.

Bill's unique prophetic spiritual gift is well-rounded and mature because of the life experiences he's had and his choice to stay in a close, tight relationship with Jesus through them all. He gives credit to the pastors who laid such a strong, firm foundation for him to follow and stay connected to Jesus Christ.

Notes

www.ingramcontent.com/pod-product-compliance
Lightning Source LLC
LaVergne TN
LVHW021349080426
835508LV00020B/2193